MTEL 90 Foundations of Reading

Teacher Certification Exam

By: Sharon A. Wynne, M.S.

XAMonline, INC.

Boston

To obtain permission(s) to use the material from this work for any purpose including workshops or seminars, please submit a written request to:

XAMonline, Inc.
21 Orient Avenue
Melrose, MA 02176
Toll Free 1-800-301-4647
Email: info@xamonline.com
Web www.xamonline.com
Fax: 1-617-583-5552

Library of Congress Cataloging-in-Publication Data

Wynne, Sharon A.
    Foundations of Reading 90: Teacher Certification / Sharon A. Wynne
    ISBN 978-1-60787-618-2
    1. Foundations of Reading 90.   2. Study Guides.   3. MTEL
    4. Teachers' Certification & Licensure.   5. Careers

Disclaimer:
The opinions expressed in this publication are the sole works of XAMonline and were created independently from the National Education Association, Educational Testing Service, or any State Department of Education, National Evaluation Systems or other testing affiliates.

Between the time of publication and printing, state specific standards as well as testing formats and website information may change that is not included in part or in whole within this product. Sample test questions are developed by XAMonline and reflect similar content as on real tests; however, they are not former tests. XAMonline assembles content that aligns with state standards but makes no claims nor guarantees teacher candidates a passing score. Numerical scores are determined by testing companies such as NES or ETS and then are compared with individual state standards. A passing score varies from state to state.

Printed in the United States of America

MTEL: Foundations of Reading (90)
ISBN: 978-1-60787-618-2

TABLE OF CONTENTS

Great Study and Testing Tips!

What to study in order to prepare for the subject assessments is the focus of this study guide but equally important is *how* you study.

You can increase your chances of truly mastering the information by taking some simple, but effective steps.

Study Tips:

1. **Some foods aid the learning process.** Foods such as milk, nuts, seeds, rice, and oats help your study efforts by releasing natural memory enhancers called CCKs (*cholecystokinin*) composed of *tryptopha*n, *choline*, and *phenylalanine*. All of these chemicals enhance the neurotransmitters associated with memory. Before studying, try a light, protein-rich meal of eggs, turkey, and fish. All of these foods release the memory enhancing chemicals. The better the connections, the more you comprehend.

Likewise, before you take a test, stick to a light snack of energy boosting and relaxing foods. A glass of milk, a piece of fruit, or some peanuts all release various memory-boosting chemicals and help you to relax and focus on the subject at hand.

2. **Learn to take great notes.** A by-product of our modern culture is that we have grown accustomed to getting our information in short doses (i.e. TV news sound bites or USA Today style newspaper articles.)

Consequently, we've subconsciously trained ourselves to assimilate information better in neat little packages. If your notes are scrawled all over the paper, it fragments the flow of the information. Strive for clarity. Newspapers use a standard format to achieve clarity. Your notes can be much clearer through use of proper formatting. A very effective format is called the *"Cornell Method."*

> Take a sheet of loose-leaf lined notebook paper and draw a line all the way down the paper about 1-2" from the left-hand edge.

> Draw another line across the width of the paper about 1-2" up from the bottom. Repeat this process on the reverse side of the page.

Look at the highly effective result. You have ample room for notes, a left hand margin for special emphasis items or inserting supplementary data from the textbook, a large area at the bottom for a brief summary, and a little rectangular space for just about anything you want.

3. <u>**Get the concept then the details.**</u> Too often we focus on the details and don't gather an understanding of the concept. However, if you simply memorize only dates, places, or names, you may well miss the whole point of the subject.

A key way to understand things is to put them in your own words. If you are working from a textbook, automatically summarize each paragraph in your mind. If you are outlining text, don't simply copy the author's words.

Rephrase them in your own words. You remember your own thoughts and words much better than someone else's, and subconsciously tend to associate the important details to the core concepts.

4. <u>**Ask Why?**</u> Pull apart written material paragraph by paragraph and don't forget the captions under the illustrations.

Example: If the heading is "Stream Erosion", flip it around to read "Why do streams erode?" Then answer the questions.

If you train your mind to think in a series of questions and answers, not only will you learn more, but it also helps to lessen the test anxiety because you are used to answering questions.

5. <u>**Read for reinforcement and future needs.**</u> Even if you only have 10 minutes, put your notes or a book in your hand. Your mind is similar to a computer; you have to input data in order to have it processed. *By reading, you are creating the neural connections for future retrieval.* The more times you read something, the more you reinforce the learning of ideas.

Even if you don't fully understand something on the first pass, *your mind stores much of the material for later recall.*

6. <u>**Relax to learn so go into exile.**</u> Our bodies respond to an inner clock called biorhythms. Burning the midnight oil works well for some people, but not everyone.

If possible, set aside a particular place to study that is free of distractions. Shut off the television, cell phone, and pager and exile your friends and family during your study period.

If you really are bothered by silence, try background music. Light classical music at a low volume has been shown to aid in concentration over other types. Music that evokes pleasant emotions without lyrics are highly suggested. Try just about anything by Mozart. It relaxes you.

7. <u>Use arrows not highlighters</u>. At best, it's difficult to read a page full of yellow, pink, blue, and green streaks. Try staring at a neon sign for a while and you'll soon see that the horde of colors obscure the message.

A quick note, a brief dash of color, an underline, and an arrow pointing to a particular passage is much clearer than a horde of highlighted words.

8. <u>Budget your study time</u>. Although you shouldn't ignore any of the material, *allocate your available study time in the same ratio that topics may appear on the test.*

Testing Tips:

1. <u>Get smart, play dumb</u>. Don't read anything into the question. Don't make an assumption that the test writer is looking for something else than what is asked. Stick to the question as written and don't read extra things into it.

2. <u>Read the question and all the choices *twice* before answering the question</u>. You may miss something by not carefully reading, and then re-reading both the question and the answers.

If you really don't have a clue as to the right answer, leave it blank on the first time through. Go on to the other questions, as they may provide a clue as to how to answer the skipped questions.

If later on, you still can't answer the skipped ones . . . *Guess.* The only penalty for guessing is that you *might* get it wrong. Only one thing is certain; if you don't put anything down, you will get it wrong!

3. <u>Turn the question into a statement</u>. Look at the way the questions are worded. The syntax of the question usually provides a clue. Does it seem more familiar as a statement rather than as a question? Does it sound strange?

By turning a question into a statement, you may be able to spot if an answer sounds right, and it may also trigger memories of material you have read.

4. <u>Look for hidden clues</u>. It's actually very difficult to compose multiple-foil (choice) questions without giving away part of the answer in the options presented.

In most multiple-choice questions you can often readily eliminate one or two of the potential answers. This leaves you with only two real possibilities and automatically your odds go to Fifty-Fifty for very little work.

5. <u>Trust your instincts</u>. For every fact that you have read, you subconsciously retain something of that knowledge. On questions that you aren't really certain about, go with your basic instincts. **Your first impression on how to answer a question is usually correct.**

6. <u>Watch the clock!</u> You have a set amount of time to answer the questions. Don't get bogged down trying to answer a single question at the expense of 10 questions you can more readily answer.

Foundations of Reading

"Any child, who doesn't learn how to read early and well, will not easily master other skills and knowledge and is unlikely to ever flourish in school or in life."
Reading is Rocket Science, American Federation of Teachers

"If our teaching of reading is to be an art, we need to draw from all we know, think and believe in order to create something beautiful."
Lucy Calkins

This guide was developed to serve the needs of test takers on the PreK-6 level who are preparing for the Foundations of Reading certification test. The quotes which introduce this work point to the crucial nature and significance of effective teaching of reading for our children and our nation's future.

This guide had a specified page limit and is designed for immediate use. The web resources and bibliographies provided will allow the reader to keep up with new research or investigate a particular strategy, referenced theorist, or term in a deeper, more detailed fashion. In addition, there is in the Appendix, a dictionary of words and terms essential to one's knowledge base as a reading teacher. Yet another study guide is a directory of key reading theorists included for your use as well.

It is my hope that this study guide will merit placement in your home or on your classroom professional library shelf for use as you begin your teaching career. Enjoy and share with your colleagues and parents, as we work together to nurture lifelong readers and writers.

Please let XAMonline know how you are able to use this guide to help you in your teacher certification experience and in your ongoing or future teaching and learning.

COMPETENCY 1.0 FOUNDATIONS OF READING DEVELOPMENT

Skill 1.1   Understand phonological and phonemic awareness

Phonological Awareness

Phonological awareness means the ability of the reader to recognize the sounds of phonemes of spoken language. This recognition includes how these sounds can be blended together, segmented (divided up), and manipulated (switched around). This awareness eventually leads to phonics, a method for decoding language by unlocking letter-sound or grapheme-phoneme relationships.

Development of phonological skills for most children begins during the pre-K years. Indeed by the age of 5, a child who has been exposed to finger plays and poetry can recognize a rhyme. Such a child can demonstrate phonological awareness by filling in the missing rhyming word in a familiar rhyme or rhymed picture book. The procedure of filling in a missing word is called the cloze procedure. It can be used in oral or print literacy activities.

One teaches children phonological awareness by directly pointing out the sounds made by letters singly (as in /b/) or in combination (as in /bl/), and to recognize individual sounds in words.

Phonological awareness skills include but are not limited to the following:

1. Rhyming and syllabification
2. Blending sounds into words—such as pic-tur-bo-k
3. Identifying beginning or initial phonemes and ending or final phonemes in short, one-syllable words
4. Breaking words down into sounds- which is also called "segmenting" words
5. Removing initial sounds, and substituting others. An example is /bat/ minus the /b/ with an /m/ substituted becomes /mat/.

The Role of Phonological Awareness in Reading Development

Instructional methods to teach phonological awareness may include any or all of the following:

1. Auditory games during which children recognize and manipulate the sounds of words, separate or segment the sounds of words, take out sounds, blend sounds, add in new sounds, or take apart sounds to recombine them in new formations.

2. Snap game- the teacher says two words. The children snap their fingers if the two words share a sound, which might be at the beginning, or end of the word. Children hear initial phonemes most easily, followed by final ones. Medial or middle sounds are most difficult for young children to discriminate. One sees this in their oral responses as well as in their invented spelling. Silence occurs if the

words share no sounds. Children love this simple game and it also helps with classroom management.

3. Language games model for children identification of rhyming words. These games help inspire children to create their own rhymes.

4. Read books that rhyme such as *Sheep in a Jeep* by Nancy Shaw or *The Fox on a Box* by Barbara Gregorich.

5. Share books with children that use alliteration (words that begin with the same sound) such as *Avalanche, A to Z.*

The Role of Phonological Processing in the Development of Individual Students

Children who are raised in homes where English is not the first language and or where standard English is not spoken, may have difficulty with hearing the difference between similar sounding words like "send" and "sent." Any child who is not in a home, day care, or preschool environment where English phonology operates, may have difficulty perceiving and demonstrating the differences between English language phonemes. If children can not hear the difference between words that "sound the same" like "grow" and "glow," they will be confused when these words appear in a print context. This confusion will of course, sadly, impact their comprehension.

Considerations for teaching phonological processing to ELL children include recognition by the teacher that what works for the English language speaking child from an English language speaking family, does not necessarily work in other languages.

Research recommends that ELL children learn to read initially in their first language. It is critical for ELL learn to speak English before being taught to read English. Research supports that oral language development lays the foundation for phonological awareness.

All phonological instruction programs must be tailored to the children's learning backgrounds. Rhymes and alliteration introduced to ELL children should be read or shared with them in their first language, if at all possible.

Struggling Readers

"Students who cannot read by age 9 are unlikely to become fluent readers and have a greater tendency to drop out"
Beth Antunez

Among the causes of reading difficulties for some children (and adults) are auditory trauma or ear infections that affect their ability to hear speech. Such children need one-on-one support with articulation and perception of different sounds. When a child says a word such as "parrot" incorrectly, repeat it back as a question with the correct. If the child "gets" the sound correctly after your question, all is well. Extra support was needed. If the child still has difficulty with pronunciation after repeated instances, then consult with a speech therapist or audiologist. Early identification of medical conditions that affect hearing is crucial to reading development.

Points to Ponder

Phonological awareness is auditory.
It does not involve print.
It begins before children have learned letter-sound relationships.
It is the basis for the successful teaching of phonics and spelling.
It can and must be taught and nurtured.
It precedes and must be in place before the alphabetic principle can be taught.

Phonemic Awareness

"The two best predictors of early reading success are alphabetic recognition and phonemic awareness."
    Marilyn Jaeger Adams

"In order to benefit from formal reading instruction, children must have a certain level of phonemic awareness . . . phonemic awareness is both a prerequisite for and a consequence of learning to read."
    Hallie Kay Yopp

Phonemic awareness is a specific skill within the broader category of phonological awareness. Probably developing fairly late, it is the knowledge that words are comprised of individual phonemes that can be blended.
Theorist Marilyn Jager Adams who researches early reading has outlined five basic types of phonemic awareness tasks.

Task 1- Ability to hear rhymes and alliteration.
For example, the children would listen to a poem, rhyming picture book or song and identify the rhyming words heard which the teacher might then record or list on chart.

Task 2- Ability to do oddity tasks (recognize the member of a set that is different [odd} among the group.
For example, the children would look at the pictures of grass, a garden, and a rose, answering, which one starts with a different sound?

Task 3 –The ability to orally blend words and split syllables.
For example, the children can say the first sound of a word and then the rest of the word and put it together as a single word.

Task 4 –The ability to orally segment words.
For example, the ability to count sounds. The child would be asked to count or clap the sounds in "hamburger."

Task 5- The ability to do phonics manipulation tasks.
For example, replace the "r" sound in rose with a "p" sound.

The Role of Phonemic Awareness in Reading Development

Children who have problems with phonics generally have not acquired or been exposed to phonemic awareness activities at home or in preschool-2. This includes extensive songs, rhymes and read-alouds.

Instructional Methods

Since the ability to distinguish between individual sounds, or phonemes, within words is a prerequisite to association of sounds with letters and manipulating sounds to blend words—a fancy way of saying "reading," the teaching of phonemic awareness is crucial to emergent literacy (early childhood K-2 reading instruction). Children need a strong background in phonemic awareness in order for phonics instruction (sound –spelling relationship-printed materials) to be effective.

Instructional methods that may be effective for teaching phonemic awareness can include:

- Clapping syllables in words

- Distinguishing between a word and a sound

- Using visual cues and movements to help children understand when the speaker goes from one sound to another

- Incorporating oral segmentation activities which focus on easily distinguished syllables rather than sounds

- Singing familiar songs (e.g. Happy Birthday, Knick Knack Paddy Wack) and replacing key words those of a different ending

- Dealing children a deck of picture cards and having them sound out the words for the pictures on their cards or calling for a picture by asking for its first and last sound.

Consideration for ELL Students

It is recommended that all teachers of reading and particularly those who are working with ELL students use meaningful, student centered, and culturally customized activities. These activities may include: language games, word walls, and poems. Some of these activities might, if possible, be initiated in the child's first language and then reiterated in English.

Assessment of Phonemic Awareness

Teachers can maintain ongoing logs and rubrics for assessment throughout the year of phonemic awareness for individual children. Such assessments would identify particular stated reading behaviors or performance standards, the date of observation of the child's behavior (in this context-phonemic activity or exercise), and comments.

The rubric or legend for assessing these behaviors might include the following descriptors:

- demonstrates or exhibits reading behavior consistently

- makes progress/strides toward this reading behavior

- has not yet demonstrated or exhibited this behavior.

Depending on the particular phonemic task the teacher models, the performance task might include:

- Saying rhyming words in response to an oral prompt

- Segmenting a word spoken by the teacher into its beginning, middle and ending sounds

- Counting correctly the number of syllables in a spoken word

Phonological awareness involves the recognition that spoken words are composed of a set of smaller units such as onsets and rimes, syllables, and sounds.

Phonemic awareness is a specific type of phonological awareness which focuses on the ability to distinguish, manipulate and blend specific sounds or phonemes within an individual word.

Think of phonological awareness as an umbrella and phonemic awareness as a specific spoke under this umbrella.

Phonics deals with printed words and the learning of sound-spelling correlations, while phonemic awareness activities are oral.

In reviewing reading research and theory, new distinctions and definitions appear often. The body of reading knowledge changes over time. The information and definitions in this guide are those accepted in the year of its publication and the time of its authoring and updating. As changes occur in accepted theories, they will be made in the guides and in the certification exams.

"If you believe that you learn to read by reading, you must learn to want to read. Reading to children, therefore models both the "how" and "why" of reading."

Helen Depree and Sandra Iversen-Early Literacy in the Classroom

"The long talk that parents have put off about the ways of the world might need to be an introduction to the facts about the English alphabet."
Terrence Moore-Ashbrook Center Fellow-Principal of Ridgeview Classical Schools in Fort Collins, Colorado

Skill 1.2 Understand Concepts of Print and the Alphabetic Principle

The Alphabetic principle is sometimes called graphophonemic awareness. This term means that written words are composed of letter (graphemes) which represent the sounds (phonemes) of written words.

Development of the Understanding that Print Carries Meaning

This understanding is demonstrated every day in the elementary classroom as the teacher holds up a selected book to read aloud to the class. The teacher explicitly and deliberately talks aloud about how to hold the book, focuses the class on looking at its cover, points to where to start reading, and sweeps her hands in the direction to begin, left to right.

When writing the morning message on the board, the teacher reminds the children that the message begins in the upper left hand corner at the top of the board to be followed by additional activities and a schedule for the rest of the day.

When the teacher invites children to make posters of a single letter such as *b* and list items in the classroom, their home, or outside which start with that letter, the children are concretely demonstrating that print carries meaning.

Strategies for Promoting Awareness of the Relationship between Spoken and Written Language

- Writing down or encoding what the children say on a language chart.

- Highlighting the uses of print products found in the classroom such as labels, yellow sticky pad notes, labels on shelves and lockers, calendars, signs, and directions.

- Reading together big-print and oversized books to teach print conventions such as directionality.

- Practicing how to handle a book: How to turn pages, to find the top and bottom of pages, and how to tell the difference between the front and back covers.

- Discussing and comparing with children the length, appearance and boundaries of specific words. For example, children can see that the names of Dan and Dora share certain letters and a similar shape.

- Having children match oral words to printed words by forming an echo chorus as the teacher reads poetry or rhymes aloud and they echo the reading.

- Having the children combine, manipulate, switch and move letters to change words.

- Working with letter cards to create messages and respond to the messages that they create.

The Role of Environmental Print in Developing Print Awareness

An environmental print book can be created by the children, which contains collaged symbols of their favorite lunch or breakfast foods. The children cut and clip symbols from the packaging of these foods and then place them in alphabetical order in their class-made book. Magazines and catalogues are another source of environmental print that is accessible with ads for child centered products. Supermarket circulars and coupons from the newspaper are also excellent for engaging children in using environmental print as reading, especially when combined with dramatic play centers or prop boxes.

What is particularly effective in using environmental print is that it immediately invites the child from ELL background into print awareness, through the familiarity of commercial logos and packaging symbols used.

Development of Book Handling Skills

Understanding the value and importance of the concepts of print for beginning readers developed out of the work of Marie Clay in New Zealand. Assessment of these skills typically occurs in kindergarten and into first grade as necessary. The following skills are part of the assessment process:

- Print carries a message – The students can demonstrate this skill even if unable to read the text by pretending to read. This may be demonstrated even if the child does not demonstrate any of the other concepts.

- Book organization – Students demonstrate an understanding of the organization of books by being able to identify the title, cover, author, left to right progression, top to bottom order, and one to one correspondence. Students may learn these skills individually as they become more familiar with books.

- Print Consistencies – This is the understanding that text is made up of letters, which then form words, which then are combined to form sentences. As the beginning reader makes these connections, they will next develop the concept of capital letters at the beginning and basic punctuation marks.

- Letter Identification– The final stage of the concepts of print assessment involves the identification of both upper- and lower- case letters. More advanced students may begin to recognize some of the most common spelling patterns in beginning texts.

Strategies for Promoting an Understanding of the Directionality of Print

In order to become proficient readers, young students need to develop a complete understanding that all print is read from left to right and top to bottom. Modeling is one of the most important strategies a teacher can use to develop this understanding in children. The use of big books, poems, and charts are strategies teachers can use in both large and small group instruction. Simple questions can engage the students to pay closer attention to these skills (i.e. "We are going to read this passage, where should I put my pointer to start reading?").

Directionality of print should also be taught during the writing process. In language experience stories, interactive writing, and Kidwriting©, the teacher can incorporate explicit modeling and instruction in these skills. Sometimes it may be necessary to provide children with a dot at the top left corner of the paper in order to provide a visual reminder of where to begin.

Techniques for Promoting the Ability to Track Print in Connected Texts

Model for children how, when pointing at words, they can start at the top and move from left to right. Tell the children that if there are more words to the sentence they are reading under the first line of print, they must go back to the left and under the previous line. Young children enjoy practicing this kinesthetic "return sweep." You might want to teach them to identify the need to do this by saying "Don't fall asleep at the page" or "Time to get to the "return sweep" stage!!" Post this saying and encourage them to singsong as they joyously take ownership of their reading. Have even beginning readers "read" through the text to find letters they recognize in the story and then share some of the text that includes these specific letters to whet their appetite for reading.

Recognition that Phonemes are Represented by Letters and Letter Pairs

As young children begin to learn to read, connections are made between the printed letters on the page and the sounds they have heard in language. Phonemic awareness activities are crucial for building this bridge. Students have engaged in many auditory activities. At this time, it is important the teacher use explicit and systematic methods to demonstrate to the students how these auditory sounds are represented on a page by letters or sometimes letter pairs. As this occurs, students can begin to decode text and move toward becoming proficient readers.

Use of Reading and Writing Strategies for Teaching Letter-sound Correspondence

When children engage in invented spelling, a common phenomenon among preschoolers, kindergartners, and even first graders, they are training themselves to listen to the sounds in words. They then try to reproduce these sounds by encoding them with letters that approximate the sounds. At first these efforts are primitive, but they follow patterns that have been documented in the research literature. Children attend first to initial, then final, and last, medial sounds. The word "cat" is spelled by many kindergartners as "c" alone, then "ct," and only after some time, as "cat." While invented spelling should be thought of as temporary and phased out around grade three, many teachers recognize that it alerts children to attend to letter-sound relationships and, once supplanted by the alphabetic principle, is a prelude to phonics.

Of course, the richest resource within the reading and writing workshop classroom for teaching and fostering the alphabetic principle lies in the use of alphabet books as anchor books for inspiring students writing. While young children in grades K-1 will do better with the one letter book authoring activity, children in grades 2 and beyond can truly be inspired and motivated by alphabet books to enhance their own reading, writing and alphabetic skills. Furthermore, use of these books which have and are being produced in a variety of formats to enhance social studies, science and mathematical themes, provide an opportunity for even young children to create a meaningful product that authenticates their content study as it enhances alphabetic skills and, of course, print awareness

Assessment throughout the Year of Graphophonemic Awareness

The teacher will want to maintain individual records of children's reading behaviors demonstrating alphabetic principle/graphophonemic awareness.

The following performance standards should be part of a record template form for each child in grades K-1 and beyond as needed (depending on ELL or special needs):

- Match all consonant and short vowel sounds.
- Read one's own name.
- Read one syllable words and high frequency words.
- Demonstrate ability to read and understand that as letters in words change, so do the sounds.
- Generate the sounds from all letters including consonant blends and long vowel patterns. Blend those different sounds into recognizable words.
- Read common sight words.
- Read common word families.
- Recognize and use knowledge of spelling patterns when reading: run/running, hop/hopping.

Any record kept of an individual child's progress should include each date of observation and some legend or rubric detailing the level of performance, standard acquisition, or mastery. Keeping accurate records assists the teacher in making quality decisions about each student's progress. These records also guide in ensuring that students are meeting each goal of the Common Core curriculum.

The following template can be used by teachers to record student progress for each child in grades K-1 and beyond as needed (depending on ELL or special needs):

Reading Progress

Skill Area	Mastered	Making Progress	Not Yet	Comments
Matches all consonant and short vowel sounds				
Reads one's own name				
Reads one syllable words and high frequency words				
Demonstrates ability to read and understand that as letters in words change, so do the sounds				
Generates the sounds from all letters including consonant blends and long vowel patterns. Blend those different sounds into recognizable words				
Reads common sight words				
Reads common word families				
Recognizes and uses knowledge of spelling patterns when reading: run/running, hop/hopping				

Any record kept of an individual child's progress should include each date of observation and some legend or rubric detailing the level of performance, standard acquisition, or mastery.

Development of Alphabetic Knowledge in Individual Students

Researchers Laura M. Justice and Helen K. Ezell (2002) evaluated alphabetic knowledge and print awareness in pre-school children from low income households. In their post-tests, children who had participated in shared reading sessions that emphasized a print focus outperformed their control group peers (other Head Start children) on three measures of print awareness: words in print, print recognition, and alphabetic knowledge.

Other researchers including Chaney (1994) have demonstrated a statistically significant and inverse relationship between household income and children's performance on measures of print awareness and the alphabetic principle.

Lonigan (1999) found that substantial group differences existed on a variety of pre literacy tasks administered to 85 preschool children from lower and middle income households. The researchers looked at environmental print, print and book reading conventions, and alphabet knowledge. Results showed that preschool children from middle income households showed significantly higher levels of skill across all print awareness tasks in comparison with preschoolers from low income households.

Obviously this data highlights the importance of extensive alphabetic knowledge activities and print awareness opportunities for some children from low income households in grades K-1 and even beyond if necessary.

Two other studies undertaken by Ezell and Justice (2000) suggested that structuring adult-child shared book reading interactions to include an explicit print awareness and alphabetic principle focus resulted in a substantial increase in children's verbal interactions with print.

This work highlights the importance of not only classroom and preschool emphasis on print awareness and alphabetic principle routines, but also the need for teachers to reach out to parents and to model for them these shared reading experiences so that family life can parallel the classroom experiences. Many schools currently have parent volunteers and reading buddy programs. Training of these volunteers, particularly in high need, low economic income status communities is certainly warranted. The Common Core curriculum can also help guide a teacher to ensure that students are meeting each necessary objective for students and his or her developmental level.

David J. Chard and Jean Osborn (1999) have reflected on the guidelines necessary for teachers to use in selecting supplemental phonics and word-recognition materials for addressing students with learning disabilities.

They note that an important way to help children with reading disabilities figure out the system underlying the printed word is leading them to understand the alphabetic principle.

For special needs children, a beginning reading program should include the following elements of alphabetic knowledge instruction:

1. A variety of alphabetic knowledge activities in which the children learn to identify and name both upper and lower case letters.
2. Games, songs, and other activities that help children to learn to name the letters quickly.
3. Writing activities that encourage children to practice the letters which they are writing.
4. A sensible sequence of letter introduction that can be adjusted to the needs of the children.

"Reading is a meaning making, problem solving activity"
Marie Clay

Skill 1.3   Understand the role of phonics in promoting reading development

Sequence of Phonics Skills

- Letter Naming
    - Lower Case Letters

- o Upper Case Letters
- Letter Sounds
  - o Continuous Sounds
  - o Stop Sounds
  - o Both Consonant and Vowel Sounds
- Short Vowels in CVC Words
- Short Vowels with Digraphs and –tch Trigraph
- Short Vowels and Consonant Blends
- Long Vowels
- Variant Vowels and Diphthongs
- R- and L- Controlled Vowels
- Multisyllabic Words

Explicit and Implicit Strategies for Teaching Phonics

Uta Frith has identified three phases which describe the progression of children's phonic learning from ages four through eight. These are:

Logographic Phase

Children recognize whole words that have significance for them such as their own names or the names of stores they frequent or products that their parents buy. Examples are McDonald's, SuperValu, and the like. Strategies which nurture development in this phase include explicit labeling of class room objects, components, furniture and materials and showing the children's names in print as often as possible. Toward the end of this phase children start to notice initial letters in words and the sounds that they represent.

Analytic Phase

During this phase the children begin to make associations between the spelling patterns in the words they know and new words-they encounter. Children in this phase of reading development are able to generalize that hat and cat are going to be read in a similar manner because they recognize that the /at/ portions of the words are the same. This is helpful with word families and can be transferred to encoding words through many activities. Some teachers find it helpful to add word families or family houses to their word walls around the room. In this way, students can begin to make these generalizations more rapidly. As the students find more complex words that fall into the family/house, they add them.

Orthographic Phase

In this phase, children recognize words almost automatically. They can rapidly identify an increasing number of words. Students are able to apply many different strategies in a seamless manner to help them decode unknown words. This may include: phonics, structural analysis, syntax, semantics, and contextual clues. Students at this level are fluent readers with good prosody. They are reading to make the shift from learning to read to reading to learn. It is a critical shift for children.

To best support these phases and the development of emergent and early readers, teachers should focus on elements of phonics learning which help children analyze words for their letters, spelling patterns, and structural components. The children need to be involved in activities in which they use what they know about words to learn new ones.

The teacher needs to build on what the children know to introduce new spelling patterns, vowel combinations, and short and long vowel investigations. The teacher must do this and be aware that these will be reintroduced again and again as needed.

Keep in mind that children's learning of phonics and other key components of reading is not linear, but rather falls back to review and then flows forward to build new understandings.

Among suggested activities to support phonics instruction to address the needs of these three phases of phonics learning are:

(These activities have specifically been provided in detail so that the educator can study them and use them in the sample constructed response questions which have been provided at the end of the guide. Since the role of phonics in promoting reading development is so crucial, it is highly likely that a constructed response question on the certification test will focus on the use of such strategies.)

Sorting Words

This activity allows children to focus closely on the specific features of words and to begin to understand the basic elements of letter sound relationships. Start with one syllable (monosyllabic) words. Have the children group them by their length, common letters, sound, and/or spelling pattern.

Prepare for the activity by writing ten to fifteen words on oaktag strips and place them randomly on the sentence strip holder. These words should come from a book previously shared in the classroom or a language experience chart.

Next begin to sort out the words with the children, perhaps by where a particular letter appears in a word. While the children sort the place of a particular letter in a given word, they should also be coached (or facilitated) by the teacher to recognize that sometimes a letter in the middle of the word can still be the last sound that we hear and that some letters at the end of a word are silent (such as "e").

Children should be encouraged to make their own categories for word sorts and to share their own discoveries as they do the word sorts. The children's discoveries should be recorded and posted in the rooms with their names so they have ownership of their phonics learning.

Spelling Pattern Word Wall

One of the understandings emergent readers come to about a word is that if they know how to read, write, and spell one word, they can write, read, and spell many other words as well.

Create in your classroom a spelling pattern word wall. The spelling word wall can be created by stapling a piece of 3" x 5" butcher block paper to the bulletin board. Then attach spelling pattern cards around the border with thumbtacks, so that the cards can be easily removed to use at the meeting area.

Once you decide on a spelling pattern for instruction, remove the corresponding card from the word wall. Then take a 1"x 3" piece of a contrasting color of butcher block paper and tape the card to the top end of a sheet the children will use for their investigation.

After the pattern is identified the children can try to come up with other words that have the same spelling pattern. The teacher can write these on the spelling pattern sheet, using a different color marker to highlight the spelling pattern within the word. The children have to add to the list until the sheet is full, which might take two days or more.

After the sheet is full, the completed spelling pattern is attached to the wall.

Letter Holder Making Words

Use a 2" x 3" piece of foam board to make a letter holder. On the front of the board, attach 16 library pockets —one for each letter from A to P. Use the back of the board to attach another 10 pockets for the rest of the alphabet.

Write the letter name on each pocket and use clear bookbinding tape to secure each row of cards with clear tape. Make twelve cards for each letter. On the front of each 2"x 6" strip, make a capital letter and on its back write that letter in lower case. Write consonants in, say, black marker and vowels in red marker.

Through use of this letter holder, children can experience how letters can be rearranged, added, or removed to make new words. They can use these cards also to focus as needed on letter sequences and to support them in recognizing spelling patterns in words.

Word Splits

Splitting compound words. Through working with compound words, children can actually experience bigger words that are often made up of smaller words. By working with five to ten compound words on oaktag cards, children can analyze letter-sound relationships and meaning.

Before children meet in a group, write five to ten words on oaktag cards and arrange them on the sentence strip holder. After the words have been read, cut each of the words into its two smaller words and randomly arrange them on the sentence strip holder. Allow the children to randomly take turns arranging the small words back into the original compound words. Also, encourage them to form new compound words. For example, if one of two original compound words is "rainbow" and the other is "dropping," the children should be able to come with "raindrop." The new words the children come up with should be written on blank oaktag cards with the names of the children who came up with them attached. In this way the children can add to their growing bank of new words and have ownership in the words that they have added.

Role of Phonics in Developing Rapid, Automatic Word Recognition, Decoding, and Reading Comprehension

To decode means to change communication signals into messages. Reading comprehension requires that the reader learn the code within which a message is written and be able to decode it to get the message.

Although effective reading comprehension requires identifying words automatically (Adams, 1990, Perfetti, 1985), children do not have to be able to identify every single word or know the exact meaning of the every word in a text to understand it. Indeed, Nagy (1988) says that, children can read a work with a high level of comprehension even if they do not fully know as many as 15 percent of the words within a given text.

Children develop the ability to decode and recognize words automatically. They then can extend their ability to decode to multi-syllabic words.

J. David Cooper (2004) and other advocates of the Balanced Literacy Approach, feel that children become literate, effective communicators and able to comprehend, by learning phonics and other aspects of word identification through the use of engaging reading texts. Engaging text, as defined by the balanced literacy group, are those texts which contain highly predictable elements of rhyme, sound patterns, and plot. Researchers, such as Jeanne Chall (1983) and Rudolf Flesch (1981), support a phonics-centered foundation before the use of engaging reading texts. This is at the crux of the phonics versus whole language/ balanced literacy/ integrated language arts, teaching of reading controversy.

It is important for the new teacher to be informed about both sides of this controversy, as well as the work of theorists who attempt to reconcile these two perspectives, such as Kenneth Goodman (1994). There are powerful arguments on both sides of this controversy, and each approach works wonderfully with some students and does not succeed with others.

This guide is designed to provide you with numerous strategies representing both approaches.

Use of Semantic and Syntactic Cues to Help Decode Words

Semantic Cues

Students will need use their base knowledge of word meanings and semantics to help them decipher unknown words or text as well as to clarify reading when it does not seem to make sense. Some prompts the teacher can use which will alert the children to semantic cues include:

- Does that sentence make sense?
- Which word in that sentence does not seem to fit?
- Why doesn't it fit?
- What word might make sense in that sentence?

Syntactic Cues

The first strategy good readers use from their own knowledge base to help determine misreading is syntactic cues. Syntactic cues use the order of words and the student's knowledge of the oral English language to help determine if what was read could be accurate. Some prompts the teacher can use to encourage and develop syntactic cues in reading include:

- You read (child's incorrect attempt). Does that sound right?
- You read (child's incorrect attempt). When we talk, do we talk that way?
- How would we say it?
- Recheck that sentence. Does it sound right the way you read it?

Specific Terminology Associated With Phonics

It is important to have a clear understanding of the terms associated with phonics. Here are some definitions, which are helpful in having a clear understanding of phonic development in children.

Phoneme – a phoneme is the smallest unit of sound in the English language. In print phonemes are represented by the letter and a slash. So, /b/ represents the sound the letter b would make.

Morpheme- a morpheme is the smallest unit of grammar in the English language. In other words, it is the smallest unit of meaning, not just sounds.

Consonant Digraph- a consonant digraph are two consonants of the English language who when placed together in a word make a unique sound, neither makes when alone. Examples: ch, th, sh, and wh.

Consonant Blend- a consonant blend is when two consonants are put together, but each retains their individual sound. The two sounds go together in a seamless manner to produce a blended sound. Examples: st, br, cl, etc.

Schwa sound- schwa sound is a vowel sound which is neutral. It typically occurs in the unaccented syllable of a word. An example would be the sound of the 'a' at the end of the word sofa. It is represented in print by an upside down e.

Development of Phonics Skills with Individual Students

In *ON SOLID GROUND* (2000), researcher and educator Sharon Taberski said that it is much harder for children from ELL backgrounds and children from homes where other English dialects are spoken to use syntactic cues to attempt to self-correct.

These children, through no fault of their own, do not have sufficient experience hearing Standard English spoken to use this cueing system as they read. The teacher should sensitively guide them through by modeling the use of syntactic and semantic cues.

Highly proficient readers can be paired as buddy tutors for ELL or special needs classroom members or to assist the resource room teacher during their reading time. They can use the CVC Game developed by Jacki Montrieth to support their peers and can even modify the game to meet the needs of classroom peers. Of course, this also offers the highly proficient reader the opportunity to do a service learning project, while still in elementary school. It also introduces the learner to another dimension of reading, the role of the reader as trainer and recruiter of other peers into the circle of readers and writers.

If the highly proficient readers are so motivated or if their teachers so desire, the peer tutors can also maintain an ongoing reading progress journal for their tutees. This will be a wonderful way to realize the goals of the reading and writing workshop.

There are many different strategies to help children who are struggling with their phonics skill development. A beginning step is to identify the area of difficulty within phonics. A simple assessment to help determine the exact area of difficulty is the CORE Phonics Survey which can be downloaded free. Once the area of deficit has been identified, small group instruction can be developed around these areas to increase specific skills.

When working on specific phonics skills, it is important to utilize decodable texts. There are numerous publishers who have available a variety of different skills and texts for use within the classroom. If students continue to struggle, it may be necessary to utilize a more specific systematic and explicit phonics program. Some examples of these include: Wilson Reading, Early Intervention Reading, and Open Court.

Skill 1.4   Understand Word Analysis Skills and Strategies

Development of Word Analysis Skills and Strategies, Including Structural Analysis

Structural analysis is a process of examining the words in the text for meaningful word units (affixes, base words, inflected endings). There are six types of word types which are formed and therefore can be analyzed using structural analysis strategies. They include:

1. Common prefixes or suffixes added to a known word ending with a consonant
2. Adding the suffix –ed to words that end with consonants
3. Compound words

4. Adding endings to words that end with the letter e
5. Adding endings to words that end with the letter y
6. Adding affixes to multisyllabic words

When teaching and using structural analysis procedures in the primary grades, teachers should remember to make sound decisions on which to introduce and teach. Keeping in mind the number of primary words in which each affix appears and how similar they are will help the teacher make the instructional process smoother and more valuable to the students.

Adding affixes to words can be started when students are able to read a list of one-syllable words by sight at a rate of approximately twenty words correct per minute. At the primary level, there is a recommended sequence for introducing affixes. The steps in this process are:

- Start by introducing the affix in the letter-sound correspondence format
- Practice the affix in isolation for a few days
- Provide words for practice which contain the affix (word lists, flash cards, etc.)
- Move from word lists to including passage reading, which include words with the affix (and some from the word lists/flash cards).

Relationship between Word Analysis Skills and Reading Comprehension

The explicit teaching of word analysis requires that the teacher pre-select words from a given text for vocabulary learning. These words should be chosen based on the storyline and main ideas of the text. The educator may even want to create a story map for a narrative text or develop a graphic organizer for an expository text. Once the story mapping and/or graphic organizing have been done, the educator can compile a list of words which relate to the storyline and/or main ideas.

The number of words that require explicit teaching should only be two or three. If the number is higher than that, the children need guided reading and the text needs to be broken down into smaller sections for teaching. Some researchers, including Tierney and Cunningham, believe that a few words should be taught as a means of improving comprehension. It is up to the educator whether the vocabulary selected for teaching needs review before reading, during reading, or after reading.

Introduce vocabulary BEFORE READING if. . .

- Children are having difficulty constructing meaning on their own. Children themselves have previewed the text and indicated words they want to know.

- The teacher has seen that there are words within the text which are definitely keys necessary for reading comprehension

- The text, itself, in the judgment of the teacher, contains difficult concepts for the children to grasp.

Introduce vocabulary DURING READING if . . .

- Children are already doing guided reading.

- The text has words which are crucial to its comprehension and the children will have trouble comprehending it, if they are not helped with the text.

Introduce vocabulary AFTER READING if. . .

- The children themselves have shared words which they found difficult or interesting

- The children need to expand their vocabulary

- The text itself is one that is particularly suited for vocabulary building.

Strategies, to support word analysis and enhance reading comprehension, include:

- Use of a graphic organizer such as a word map
- Semantic mapping
- Semantic feature analysis
- Hierarchical and linear arrays
- Preview in context
- Contextual redefinition
- Vocabulary self-collection
- (Note that these terms are in the Glossary.)

Identification of Common Morphemes, Prefixes, and Suffixes

The term list below is generally recognized as the key structural analysis components.

Root Words

This is a word from which another word is developed. The second word can be said to have its "root" in the first, such as *vis, to see,* in visor or vision. This structural component can be illustrated by a tree with roots to display the meaning for children. Children may also want to literally construct root words using cardboard trees to create word family models.

Base Words
These are stand-alone linguistic units which cannot be deconstructed or broken down into smaller words. For example, in the word *re-tell*, the base word is "tell."

Contractions

These are shortened forms of two words in which a letter or letters have been deleted. These deleted letters have been replaced by an apostrophe.

Prefixes

These are beginning units of meaning which can be added (the vocabulary word for this type of structural adding is "affixed") to a base word or root word. They can not stand alone. They are also sometimes known as "bound morphemes" meaning that they can not stand alone as a base word. Examples are *re-, un-,* and *mis-.*

Suffixes

These are ending units of meaning which can be "affixed" or added on to the ends of root or base words. Suffixes transform the original meanings of base and root words. Like prefixes, they are also known as "bound morphemes," because they can not stand alone as words. Examples are *-less, -ful,* and *-tion.*

Compound Words

These occur when two or more base words are connected to form a new word. The meaning of the new word is in some way connected with that of the base word. Examples are *firefighter, newspaper,* and *pigtail.*

Inflectional Endings

These are types of suffixes that impart a new meaning to the base or root word. These endings in particular change the gender, number, tense, or form of the base or root words. Just like other suffixes, these are also termed "bound morphemes." Examples are *–s* or *-ed.*

Techniques for Identifying Compound Words

The teaching of compound words should utilize structural analysis techniques. (See above section on structural analysis).

Here are some other strategies for helping students to identify and read compound words.

- Use songs and actions to help children understand the concept that compound words are two smaller words joined together to make one bigger word
- Use games like concentration, memory and go fish for students to practice reading compound words
- Use word sorts to have students distinguish between compound words and non-examples of compound words

Identification of Homographs

Homographs are words that are spelled the same but have different meanings. A subgroup within this area includes words that are spelled the same, have different meanings, and are pronounced differently. Some examples of homographs include:

- Lie
- Tear
- Bow
- Fair
- Bass

Contextual Redefinition

This strategy encourages children to use the context more effectively by presenting them with sufficient context BEFORE they begin reading. It models for the children the use of contextual clues to make informed guesses about word meanings.

To apply this strategy, the teacher should first select unfamiliar words for teaching. No more than two or three words should be selected for direct teaching. The teacher should then write a sentence in which there are sufficient clues supplied for the child to successfully figure out the meaning. Among the types of context clues the teacher can use are: compare/contrast, synonyms, and direct definition.

Then the teacher should present the words only on the experiential chart or as letter cards. Have the children pronounce the words. As they pronounce them, challenge them to come up with a definition for each word. After more than one definition is offered, encourage the children to decide as a whole group what the definition is. Write down their agreed upon definition with no comment as to its accurate meaning.

Then share with the children the contexts (sentences the teacher wrote with the words and explicit context clues). Ask that the children to read the sentences aloud. Then have the students come up with a definition for each word. Make certain that as they present their definitions, the teacher does not comment. Ask that they justify their definitions by making specific references to the context clues in the sentences. As the discussion continues, direct the children's attention to their previously agreed-upon definition of the word. Facilitate their discussing the differences between their guesses about the word when they saw only the word itself and their guesses about the word when they read it in context. Finally have the children check their use of context skills to correctly define the word by using a dictionary.

Development of Word Analysis Skills by Individual Students

This type of direct teaching of word definitions is useful when the children have dictionary skills and the teacher is aware of the fact that there are not sufficient clues about the words in the context to help the students define it. In addition, struggling readers and students from ELL backgrounds may benefit tremendously from being walked through this process that highly proficient and successful readers apply automatically

By using this strategy, the teacher can also "kid watch" and note the students' prior knowledge as they guess the word in isolation. The teacher can also actually witness and hear how various students use context skills.

Through their involvement in this strategy, struggling readers gain a feeling of community as they experience the ways in which their struggles and guesses resonate with other peers' responses to the text.

"Knowledge of vocabulary will not guarantee vocabulary success, but lack of vocabulary knowledge can ensure failure."
Andrew Biemiller (2003)

COMPETENCY 2.0 DEVELOPMENT OF READING COMPREHENSION

Skill 2.5   Understand Vocabulary Development

The Relationship between Oral and Written Vocabulary Development and Reading Comprehension

Biemiller's (2003) research documents that those children entering 4th grade with significant vocabulary deficits demonstrate increasing reading comprehension problems. Evidence shows that these children do not catch up, but rather continue to fall behind.

Strategy One: Word Map Strategy

This strategy is useful for children grades 3-6 and beyond. The target group of children for this strategy includes those who need to improve their independent vocabulary acquisition abilities. The strategy is essentially teacher-directed learning where children are "walked through" the process. They are helped by the teacher to identify the type of information that makes a definition. They are also assisted in using context clues and background understanding to construct meaning.

The word map graphic organizer is the tool teachers use to complete this strategy with children. Word map templates are available online from the Houghton Mifflin web site and from READWRITETHINK, the web site of the NCTE (see webliography section). The word map helps the children to visually represent the elements of a given concept.

The children's literal articulation of the concept can be prompted by three key questions: What is it? What is it like? What are some examples?

For instance, the word "oatmeal" might yield a word map with "What?", and in a rectangular box a hot cereal you eat in the morning, "What is it like?"; hot, mushy, salty, "What are some examples?",   instant oatmeal you make in a minute, apple-flavor oatmeal, Irish Oatmeal.

The procedure to be used in sharing this strategy with children is to select three concepts the children are familiar with. Then show them the template of a word map. Tell them that the three questions asked on the map and the boxes to fill in beneath them helps readers and writers to see what they need to know about a word. Next, help the children to complete at least two word maps for two of the three concepts that were pre-selected. Then have the children select a concept of their own to map either independently or in a small group. As the final task for this first part of the strategy, have the children, in teams or individually, write a definition for at least one of the concepts using the key things about it listed on the map. Have the children share these definitions aloud and talk about how they used the word maps to help them with the definitions.

For the next part of this strategy, the teacher should pick up an expository text or a textbook the children are already using to study mathematics, science or social studies. The teacher should either locate a short excerpt where a particular concept is defined or use the content to write model passages of definition on his/her own.

After the passages are selected or authored, the teacher should duplicate them. Then they should be distributed to the children along with blank word map templates. The children should be asked to read each passage and then to complete the word map for the concept in each passage. Finally, have the children share the word maps they have developed for each passage. Give them a chance to explain how they used the word in the passage to help them fill out their word map. End by telling them that the three components of the concept-class, description, example- are just three of the many components for any given concept.

This strategy has assessment potential because the teacher can literally see how the students understand specific concepts by looking at their maps and hearing their explanations. The maps the students develop on their own demonstrate whether they have really understood the concepts in the passages. This strategy serves to ready students for inferring word meanings on their own. By using the word map strategy, children develop concepts of what they need to know to begin to figure out an unknown word on their own. It assists the children in grades 3 and beyond to connect prior knowledge with new knowledge.

This word map strategy can be adapted by the teacher to suit the specific needs and goals of instruction. Illustrations of the concept and the comparisons to other concepts can be included in the word mapping for children grades 5 and beyond. This particular strategy is also one that can be used with a research theme in other content areas.

Strategy Two: Preview in Context

This is a direct teaching strategy which allows the teacher to guide the students as they examine words in context prior to reading a passage. Before beginning the strategy, the teacher selects only two or three key concept words. Then the teacher reads carefully to identify passages within the text that evidence strong context clues for the word.

Then the teacher presents the word and the context to the children. As the teacher reads aloud, the children follow along. Once the teacher has finished the read aloud, the children re-read the material silently. After the silent re-reading, the children will be coached by the teacher to a definition of one of the key words selected for study. This is done through a child-centered discussion. As part of the discussion, the teacher asks questions which get the children to activate their prior knowledge and to use the contextual clues to figure out the correct meaning of the selected key words. Make certain that the definition of the key concept word is finally made by the children.

Next, help the children to begin to expand the word's meaning. Do this by having them consider the following for the given key concept word: synonyms, antonyms, other contexts or other kinds of stories/texts where the word might appear. This is the time to have the children check their responses to the challenge of identifying word synonyms and antonyms by having them go to the thesaurus or the dictionary to confirm their responses. In addition, have the children place the synonyms or antonyms they find in their word boxes or word journals. The recording of their findings will guarantee them ownership of the words and deepen their capacity to use contextual clues.

The main point to remember in using this strategy is that it should only be used when the context is strong. It will not work with struggling readers who have less prior knowledge. Through listening to the children's responses as the teacher helps them to define the word and its potential synonyms and antonyms, the teacher can assess their ability to successfully use context clues. The key to this simple strategy is that it allows the teacher to draw the child out and to grasp through the child's responses the individual child's thinking process. The more talk from the child the better.

The Role of Systematic, Noncontextual Vocabulary Strategies

Strategy One: Hierarchical and Linear Arrays

The very complexity of the vocabulary used in this strategy description, may be unnerving for the teacher. Yet this strategy included in the Cooper (2004) literacy instruction is really very simple once it is outlined directly for children.

By using the term "hierarchical and linear" arrays, Cooper really is talking about how some words are grouped based on associative meanings. The words may have a "hierarchical" relationship to one another. For instance, an undergraduate or a first grader is lower in the school hierarchy than the graduate student and second grader. Within an elementary school, the fifth grader is at the top of the hierarchy and the pre K or kindergartener is at the bottom of the hierarchy. By the way, the term for this strategy obviously need not be explained in this detail to K-3 children, but might be shared with some grade and age appropriate modifications with children in grades 3 and beyond. It will enrich their vocabulary development and ownership of arrays they create.

Words can have a linear relationship to one another in that they run a spectrum from bad to good-for example from K-3 experiences, pleased-happy-overjoyed. These relationships can be displayed in horizontal boxes connected with dashes. Below is another way to display hierarchical relationships.

Once you get past the seemingly daunting vocabulary words, the arrays turn out to be another neat, graphic organizer tool which can help children "see" how words relate to one another.

To use this graphic organizer, the teacher should pre-select a group of words from a read aloud or from the children's writing. Show the children how the array will look using arrows for the linear array and just straight lines for the hierarchy. In fact invite some children up to draw the straight hierarchy lines as it is presented, so they have a role in developing even the first hierarchical model.

Do one hierarchy array and one linear array with the pre selected word with the children. Talk them through filling out (or helping the teacher to fill out) the array. After the children have had their own successful experience with arrays, they can select the words from their independent texts or familiar, previously read favorites to study. They will also need to decide which type of array, hierarchical or linear, is appropriate. For 5th and 6th graders, this choice can and should be voiced using the now "owned" vocabulary words "hierarchical array" and "linear array."

This strategy is best used after reading, since it will help the children to expand their word banks.

Contextual Vocabulary Strategies

Vocabulary Self-Collection. This strategy is one in which children, even on the emergent level from grade 2 and up, take responsibility for their learning. It is also by definition, a student centered strategy, which demonstrates student ownership of their chosen vocabulary.

This strategy is one that can be introduced by the teacher early in the year, perhaps even the first day or week. The format for self-collection can then be started by the children. It may take the form of a journal with photocopied template pages. It can be continued throughout the year.

To start, ask the children to read a required text or story. Invite them to select one word for the class to study from this text or story. The children can work individually, in teams or in small groups. The teacher can also do the self-collecting so that this becomes the joint effort of the class community of literate readers. Tell the children that they should select words which particularly interest them or which are unique in some way.

After the children have had time to make their selections and to reflect on them, make certain that they have time to share them with their peers as a whole class. When each child shares the word which he or she has selected, have them provide a definition for the word. Each word that is given should be listed on a large experiential chart or even in a BIG BOOK format, if that is age and grade appropriate. The teacher should also share the word he or she selected and provide a definition. The teacher's definition and sharing should be somewhere in the middle of the children's recitations.

The dictionary should be used to verify the definitions. When all the definitions have been checked, a final list of child-selected (and single teacher-selected) words should be made.

Once this final list has been compiled, the children can record it in their word journals or they may opt to record only those words they find interesting in their individual journals. It is up to the teacher at the onset of the vocabulary self-collection activity to decide whether the children have to record all the words on the final list or can eliminate some. The decision made at the beginning by the teacher must be adhered to throughout the year.

To further enhance this strategy, children, particularly those in grades 3 and beyond, can be encouraged to use their collected words as part of their writings or to record and clip the appearance of these words in newspaper stories or online. This type of additional recording demonstrates that the child has truly incorporated the word into his/her reading and writing. It also habituates children to be lifelong readers, writers, and researchers.

One of the nice things about this simple but versatile strategy is that it works equally well with either expository or narrative texts. It also provides children with an opportunity to use the dictionary.

Assessment is built into the strategy. As the children select the word for the list, they share how they used contextual clues and through the children's response to the definitions offered by their peers, their prior knowledge can be assessed.

What is most useful about this strategy is that it documents that children can learn to read and write by reading and writing. The children take ownership of the words in the self-collection journals and that can also be the beginning of writer observation journals as they include their own writings. They also use the word lists as a start for writers' commonplace books. These books are filled with newspaper, magazine, and functional document clippings using the journal words.

This activity is a good one for demonstrating the balanced literacy belief that vocabulary study works best when the words studied are chosen by the child.

The Relationship between Oral Vocabulary and the Process of Identifying and Understanding Written Words

One way to explore the relationship between oral vocabulary and the comprehension of written words is through the use of Oral Records (which are discussed at length in the appendix).

In *On Solid Ground: Strategies for Teaching Reading K-3*, Sharon Taberski (2000) discusses how oral reading records can be used by the K-3 teacher to assess how well children are using cueing systems. She notes that the running record format can also show visual depictions for the teacher of how the child "thinks" as the child reads. The notation of miscues in particular shows how a child "walks through" the reading process. They indicate if and in what ways the child may require "guided" support in understanding the words he or she reads aloud. Taberski notes that when children read they need to think about several things at once. First, they must consider whether what they are reading makes sense (semantic or meaning cues). Next, they must know whether their reading "sounds right" in terms of Standard English (syntactic and structural cues). Third, they have to weigh whether their oral language actually and accurately matches the letters the words represent (visual or graphophonic cues).

In taking the running record and having the opportunity first-hand to listen to the children talk about the text, the teacher can analyze the relationship between the child's oral language and word comprehension. Information from the running record provides the teacher with a road map for differentiated cueing system instruction.

For example, when a running record is taken, a child often makes a mistake but then self-corrects. The child may select from various cueing systems when he or she self-corrects. These include: "M" for meaning, "S" for syntax, and "V" for visual. The use of a visual cue means that the child is drawing on his or her knowledge of spelling patterns. Of course, Tabereski cautions that any relationship between oral language and comprehension that the teacher draws from an examination of the oral-reading records, must be drawn using a series of three or more of the child's oral reading records, taken over time, not just one.

A teacher can review children's running records over time to note their pattern of miscues and which cues they have the greatest tendency to use in their self-corrections. Whichever cueing system the children use to the greatest extent, it is necessary for the teacher to offer support in also using the other cueing systems to construct correct meaning. Taberski suggests that while assessing running records to determine the relationship between oral language and meaning, the children read from "just right" books.

Strategies for Promoting Oral Language Development and Language Comprehension

Read-Alouds (This is the corner piece of the balanced literacy approach for teaching reading. Therefore it is advised that the teacher candidate and new teacher read this material carefully. This may well appear as an essay topic in the Constructed Response section).

Comments:

Within the context of the Balanced Literacy Approach and the Literacy Block, the Read Aloud is part of the Whole Class Activities. The book selected should be one taken from the classroom library, which is appropriate for a read aloud. Before reading the book to the class, the teacher needs to be familiar with it. The teachers should also "plan" or at least "know" what nuances of content, style, rhythm, and vocabulary that will be emphasized in the reading.

In addition, specifically for the younger grades, the teacher should select a text which also enhances the development of phonemic awareness. This might include a text that can be used to teach rhyming, alliteration, or poetry.

Sometimes, read-aloud texts are selected for their tie-ins with the science, social studies and mathematics curriculum.

Generally, teachers aim to teach one strategy during the read-aloud, which the children will practice in small groups or independently. Among these strategies for the first grader could be print strategies and talking about books.

As the teacher reads aloud, the teachers' voice quality should highlight his or her enjoyment of the read-aloud and involvement with its text. Often in a balanced literacy classroom, the teacher reads from a specially decorated Reader's Chair, as do the guest readers. This chair's decorativeness, complete with comfortable throwback pillows or rocking chair style frame, is meant to set an atmosphere that will promote the children's engagement in and love for lifelong reading.

The balanced literacy approach also advocates that teachers select books which children will enjoy hearing read aloud. Particularly accessible texts for the elementary school classroom read-alouds are collections of poetry.

Teachers must allow time for discussion during and after each Read Aloud period. After the children have made comments, the teacher should also talk about the reading.

Knowledge of Common Sayings, Proverbs and Idioms

Strategy: The Fortune Cookie Strategy (Reissman, 1994). Grades 3 and up

Distribute just before snack (fortune cookies) to the children. Have them eat the cookies and then draw their attention to the fortunes which are enclosed.

First, the teacher will model by reading aloud and sharing his/her own fortune. After reading the fortune aloud, the teacher will explain what the fortune means using its vocabulary as a guide. Finally the teacher can share whether or not the teacher agrees with the statement made in the fortune.

Children can either volunteer to share their fortunes or each can read the fortune aloud, explain the saying and tell whether he or she agrees with the proverb.

Next, children can be asked to go home and interview their parents or community members to get family proverbs and common sayings.

Once the children return with the sayings and proverbs, they can each share them and explain their meaning. The class as a whole can discuss to what extent these sayings are true for everyone. Proverbs and Sayings can become part of a word wall or be included in a special literacy center. The teacher can create fill in, put together, and writing activities to go with the proverbs. They tie in nicely with cultural study on the grade 3-6 level including Asian, Latin American, and African nations.

What makes proverbs particularly effective for vocabulary development are the limited number of words in their texts and the fact these short texts allow for guided and facilitated reading instruction.

This strategy also highlights in a positive way the uniqueness and commonality of the family proverbs which are contributed by children from ELL backgrounds. If possible their proverbs can also be posted in their native languages as well as in English.

Knowledge of Foreign Words and Abbreviations Commonly Used in English (e.g. RSVP)

Strategy: RSVP your foreign language in English literacy

Of course, the English language is replete with abbreviations that are shortened forms of words from other languages. Not only can this be used for expanding children's vocabulary and writing variety; but also it can help to positively highlight the bilingual and sometimes trilingual abilities of ELL students.

The teacher should develop a word strip mix and match game with commonly found foreign words and abbreviations. These items should, if possible, be cut out of newspapers and flyers to highlight their authenticity as part of every day life objects. Among those common words and abbreviations might be: perfume, liqueur (chocolate, of course), latte, cappuccino, pannini, brioche, latkes, and the like. Food, local Starbucks, coffee houses, and bakeries are excellent sources of these abbreviations. To get sufficient material to cut out to start the game, just get an extra Sunday newspaper or pick up a few circulars from a large supermarket.

Model for the children how to play the game and find out the common words or abbreviations meaning and foreign derivation using the dictionary.

Next have the children as a whole class or in small groups, work to identify the derivations of the foreign words and even map them on a world map.

As part of additional, foreign word center activities, children can opt among a number of choices. These can include: maintaining a BIG BOOK OF FOREIGN WORDS or ABBREVIATIONS, to which many contribute, using the weekly food circulars and collecting labels with foreign words which can then be collaged with an accompanying product list, authoring stories and true accounts featuring as many foreign words as possible.

What is productive about this strategy is that it enhances vocabulary development while it also highlights the extent to which the English language as spoken, used and written in the United States currently, is embedded with foreign language words and terms. This of course, makes the native language talents of the ELL child positive and important ones.

Extending a Reader's Understanding of Familiar Words

Dictionary Use:

Dictionaries are useful for spelling, writing, and reading. It is very important to initially expose and habituate students to enjoy using the dictionary.

Cooper (2004) suggests that the following be kept in mind as the teacher of grades K-6 introduces and then habituates children to a lifelong fascination with the dictionary and vocabulary acquisition.

Requesting or suggesting that children look up a word in the dictionary should be an invitation to a wonderful exploration, not a punishment or busy work that has no reference to their current reading assignment.

Model the correct way to use the dictionary for children even as late as the third –sixth grade. Many have never been taught proper dictionary skills. The teacher needs to demonstrate to the children that as an adult reader and writer, he or she routinely and happily uses the dictionary and learns new information that makes him or her better at reading and writing.

Cooper believes in beginning dictionary study as early as kindergarten and this is now very possible because of the proliferation of lush picture dictionaries which can be introduced at that grade level. He also suggests that children not only look at these picture dictionaries, but also begin to make dictionaries of their own at this grade level filled with pictures and beginning words. As children join the circle of lexicographers, they will begin to see themselves as compilers and users of dictionaries. Of course, this will support their ongoing vocabulary development.

In early grade levels, use of the dictionary can nicely complement the children's mastery of the alphabet. They should be given whole class and small group practice in locating words.

As the children progress with their phonetic skills, the dictionary can be used to show them phonetic re-spelling using the pronunciation key.

Older children in grades 3 and beyond need explicit teacher demonstrations and practice in the use of guide words. They also need to begin to learn about the hierarchies of various word meanings. In the upper grades, children should also explore using special content dictionaries and glossaries in the backs of their books.

Strategies for Promoting Comprehension across the Curriculum by Expanding Knowledge of Content Area Vocabulary

Key Words

Cooper (2004) feels that it is up to the teacher to preview the content area text to identify the main ideas. Then the teacher should compile a list of terms related to the content thrust. These terms and words become part of the key concepts list.

Next, the teacher sees which of the key concept words and terms are already defined in the text. These will not require direct teaching. Words for which children have sufficient skills to determine their meaning through base, root, prefixes or suffixes, also will not require direct teaching.

Instruction in the remaining key words, which should not be more than two or three in number, can be provided before, during or after reading. If students have previewed the content area and identified those words they need support on, the instruction should be provided before reading. Instruction can also easily be provided as part of guided reading support. After reading support is indicated, the text offers the children an opportunity to enrich their own vocabularies.

Having children work as a whole class or in small groups on a content specific dictionary for a topic regularly covered in their grade level social studies, science, or mathematics, curriculum offers an excellent collaborative opportunity for children to design a dictionary/word resource that can celebrate their own vocabulary learning. Such a resource can then be used with the next year's classes as well.

Development of Vocabulary Knowledge and Skills in Individual Students

Hierarchical and linear array vocabulary development strategies lend themselves well to support the struggling learners or second language learners. The use of the arrays allows these learners to use a visual format to "see" and diagram word relationships. Furthermore the diagrams are easy to make, and they can be illustrated. With sufficient support and modeling, many special needs children can do simple linear and hierarchical arrays on their own. The arrays can also be attractively displayed in resource rooms and in regular education classrooms as a demonstration of these individual students' ownership of their words.

English Language Learners should first capably demonstrate their capacity to fill out hierarchical and linear arrays in their native language and then can work with this same format to hone their English Language vocabulary development. Their native language hierarchical relationships and arrays can be displayed in their general education classrooms. Teachers may also want to encourage children grades 3 and beyond to make connections between some of the native, other than English, words and words derived from them in English. This could be a rich "buddy" (ELL child and native English Language speaker) investigation or it could be one for ELL children alone. At any rate, use of the array with the ELL child's native language makes that child a second language vocabulary owner which immediately includes the child positively in ongoing vocabulary development.

Cooper (2004) suggests that teachers who have children from different language backgrounds use any unscheduled or "extra" time that emerges for read-alouds.

Using the Semantic Feature Analysis Grid

Highly proficient readers can be asked to help same grade peers or better yet younger peers with their word analysis skills by having them work with these struggling readers on filling out teacher developed semantic analysis grids. Some 5th and 6th grade highly proficient readers may also evidence the aptitude and desire to create their own semantic analysis grids for their peer or younger peer tutees. In this way, highly proficient readers can gain insights into the field of teaching reading at an early age and younger struggling readers can have the edge taken off their struggles by working with a peer or an older student. For both individual students the experience is one that promotes and celebrates word analysis skills and nurtures the concept of a literate and caring community of readers.

ELL students can also add in deliberate items to the categories which reflect their cultures. For instance, Latino children can add in plantains and guava to the fruits their non-Latino peers might list. This provides the ELL learners with an opportunity to enrich the knowledge base of their peer's subject category inventory and puts them in a positive spotlight. The easy notations on the grid make it accessible for even ELL children with limited English language writing and speaking capacities.

Special Needs learners can benefit from the grid. It can be developed by teachers, paraprofessionals, and tutors. It can be notated by the children themselves. They can also illustrate it. It can be posted or kept in the word center. The grid provides these learners who are often spatial learners with a concrete demonstration of their word analysis achievement.

Biemiller's research indicates that the listening vocabulary for a 6th grader who tests at the 25 percentile in reading is equivalent to that attained by the 75th percentile 3rd grader. This deficit in vocabulary presents a formidable challenge for the 6th grader to succeed, not only on reading tests, but in various content subjects in elementary school and beyond.

"If we encounter a man of rare intellect, we should ask him what books he reads."
Ralph Waldo Emerson

Skill 2.6   Understand How to Apply Reading Comprehension Skills to Imaginative/literary Texts

Knowledge of Reading as a Process to Construct Meaning

If there were two words synonymous with reading comprehension as far as the balanced literacy approach is concerned, they would be "constructing meaning."

Cooper, Taberski, Strickland, and other key theorists and classroom teachers conceptualize the reader as interacting with the text and bringing his/her prior knowledge and experience to it. Writing is interlaced with reading and is a mutually integrative and supportive parallel process. Hence the division of literacy learning by the balanced literacy folks into reading workshop and writing workshop, with the same anchor "readings" or books being used for both.

Consider the sentence, "The test booklet was white with black print, but very scary looking."

According to the idea of constructing meaning as the reader read this sentence, the schemata (generic information stored in the mind) of tests the reader had experienced was activated by the author's notion that tests are scary. Therefore the ultimate meaning that the reader derives from the page is from the reader's own responses and experiences coupled with the ideas the author presents. The reader constructs a meaning that reflects the author's intent and also the reader's response to that intent.

It is also to be remembered that generally readings are fairly lengthy passages, composed of paragraphs which in turn are composed of more than one sentence. With each successive sentence, and every new paragraph, the reader refocuses. The schemata are reconsidered, and a new meaning is constructed.

Knowledge of levels of reading comprehension and strategies for promoting comprehension of imaginative literary texts at all levels

Sharon Taberski (2000) recommends that initially strategies for promoting comprehension of imaginative literary texts be done with the whole class.

Here are Taberski's four main strategies for promoting comprehension of imaginative literary texts. She feels that if repeated sufficiently during the K-3 years and even if introduced as late as grade 4, these strategies will even serve the adult lifelong reader in good stead.

Strategy One: "Stopping to Think" – reflecting on the text as a whole.

As part of this strategy, the reader is challenged to come up with the answer to these three questions:

- What do I think is going to happen? (Inferential)
- Why do I think this is going to happen? (Evaluative and inferential)
- How can I prove that I am right by going back to the story? (Inferential)

Taberski recommends that teachers introduce these key strategies with books that can be read in one sitting and recommends the use of picture books for these instructive strategies. Note that while literal questions have answers that can be found directly in a book, an inferential question must be answered by a judgment based on evidence. If, for example, on one page we see a cake accompanied by the rear legs of a dog jumping out of the window, children can infer who stole part of the cake. Evaluative questions ask that children state an opinion or make a judgment, as in "Do you think the party was ruined by this?"

Taberski also suggests that books which are read aloud and used for this strategy also contain a strong storyline, some degree of predictability, a text that invites discussion and a narrative with obvious stopping points.

Strategy Two: story mapping, for promoting comprehension of imaginative/literary texts.

For stories to suit this strategy, they should have distinct episodes, few characters and clear-cut problems to solve. In particular, Taberski tries to use a story where a single, central problem or issue is introduced at the beginning of the story and then resolved or at least followed through by the close of the story. To make a story map of a particular story, Taberski divides the class into groups and asks one group of children to illustrate the "Characters" in the book. Another group of children are asked to draw the "Setting," while a third and fourth group of children tackle "Problem " and "Resolution." The story map may also help children hold together their ideas for writing in the writing workshop as they take their reading of an author's story to a new level.

Strategy Three: The Character Mapping strategy also used by Taberski focuses the children as readers on the ways in which the main character's personal traits can determine what will happen in the story. Character mapping works best when the character is a non-stereotypical individual, has been featured perhaps in other books by the same author, has a personality that is somewhat predictable, and is capable of changing behavior as a consequence of what happens. Using writing to share, deepen, and expand understanding of literary texts is a cornerstone of the balanced literacy approach.

Strategy Four: Taberski advocates reading sections of stories aloud and then having the teacher pause to reflect on what's happened in the story and model writing down a response to it. The teacher can use a chart to record his/her response to the events or characters of a particular story being read and the children can contribute their comments as well. Later on, the children can start reflective reader's notebooks or journals recording their reactions to their readings independently.

The best types of texts for this type of response are those that relate to age appropriate issues for young children (i.e. homework, testing, bullies, and friendship), a plot that can be interpreted in different ways, a text that is filled with questions, and a text full of suspense or wonder.

Development of Literary Response Skills

Literary response skills are dependent on prior knowledge, schemata and background. Schemata (the plural of schema) are those structures which represent concepts stored in our memory.

Without schemata and experiences to call upon as they read, children have little ability to comprehend. Of course, the reader's schemata and prior knowledge have more influence on the comprehension of plot or character information that is implied rather than directly stated.

Prior Knowledge

Prior knowledge can be defined as all of an individual's prior experiences, learning, and development which precede his/her entering a specific learning situation or attempting to comprehend a specific text. Sometimes prior knowledge can be erroneous or incomplete. Obviously, if there are misconceptions in a child's prior knowledge, these must be corrected so that the child's overall comprehension skills can continue to progress. Prior knowledge of children includes their accumulated positive and negative experiences both in and out of school.

These might come from wonderful family travels, watching television, visiting museums and libraries, to visiting hospitals, prisons and surviving poverty. Whatever the prior knowledge that the child brings to the school setting, the independent reading and writing the child does in school immeasurably expands his/her prior knowledge and hence broadens his/her reading comprehension capabilities.

The teacher must consider as he/she prepares to begin any imaginative/literary text the following about the students' level of prior knowledge:

1. What prior knowledge needs to be activated for the text, theme or for the writing to be done successfully?
2. How independent are the children in using strategies to activate their prior knowledge?

Holes and Roser (1987) have suggested techniques for activating prior knowledge before starting an imaginative/literary text:

- Free Recall: Tell us what you know about...

- Unstructured Discussion: Let's talk about...

- Structured Question: Who exactly was Jane Aviles in the life of the hero of the story?

- Word Association: When you hear these words--hatch, elephant, who, think-- What author do you think of?

- Recognition: Mulberry Street...What author comes to mind?

- Previewing and predicting and story mapping are also excellent strategies for activating prior knowledge.

Development of Literary Analysis Skills

There are many exciting ways to sensitize and to teach children about the features and formats of different literary genres. First and foremost, the teacher should choose fine children's literature as the basis for teaching literary analysis skills. Typically for younger children, teachers turn to picture books. The best-illustrated picture book published in the U.S. each year wins the Caldecott award, named for Randolph Caldecott who was a 19th century English illustrator. There is one winning book selected yearly as well as one, two, or three Honor Books. Teachers cannot go wrong in selecting "Caldecott books" to share with children. In recent years, more and more picture books are being written for older children as well.

Another award in children's literature which is critically important is the Newbery Medal, presented for the most distinguished children's book written by a U.S. author in any given year. The Newbery award-winning books tend to be suitable for intermediate and middle-level children. The award is named for John Newbery, an 18th century English bookseller. Like the Caldecott awards, there is one "big" winner as well as several honor books selected each year.

Use of Comprehension Strategies Before, During, and After Reading

Cooper (2004), Taberski (2000), Cox (2005) and other researchers recommend a broad array of comprehension strategies before, during, and after reading.

Cooper (2004) suggests a broad range of classroom posters on the walls plus explicit instruction to give children prompts to monitor their own reading. An example follows:

My Strategic Reading Guide

1. Do I infer/predict important information, use what I know, think about what may happen or what I want to learn?
2. Can I identify important information about the story elements?
3. Do I generate questions and search for the answers?
4. Does this make sense to me? Does this help me meet my purpose in reading?
5. If lost, do I remember fix-ups?
6. Re-read, read further ahead, look at the illustrations, ask for help, and think about the words, and evaluate what I have read.
7. Do I remember to think about how the parts of the stories that I was rereading came together?

Storyboard panels, which are used by comic strip artists and by those artists who do advertising campaigns as well as television and film directors, are perfect for engaging children K-6 in a variety of comprehension strategies before, during, and after reading. They can storyboard the beginning of a story, read aloud, and then storyboard its predicted middle or end. Of course, after they experience or read the actual middle or ending of the story, they can compare and contrast what they produced with its actual structure. They can play familiar literature identification games with a buddy or as part of a center by storyboarding one key scene or characters from a book and challenging a partner or peer to identify the book and characters correctly.

Use of Oral Language Activities to Promote Comprehension

Retelling

Retelling needs to be very clearly defined so that the child reader does not think that the teacher wants him or her to spill the WHOLE story back in the retelling. A child should be able to talk comfortably and fluently about the story he or she has just read. He or she should be able to tell the main things that have happened in the story.

When a child retells a story to a teacher, the teacher needs ways to help him or her assess the child's understanding. Ironically, the teacher can use some of the same strategies he or she suggests to the child to assess the child's understanding of a book which is not familiar to the teacher. These strategies include: back cover reading, scanning the table of contents, looking at the pictures, and reading the book jacket.

If the child can explain how the story turned out and provide examples to support these explanations, try not to interrupt him or her with too many questions.

Children can use the text of the book to reinforce what they are saying and they can even read from it if they wish. It is also important to note that some children need to re-read the text twice and their re-reading of it is out of enjoyment.

When the teacher plans to use the retelling as a way of assessing the child, then the following ground rules have to be set and made clear to the child. The teacher explains the purpose of the retelling to determine how well the child is reading at the outset of the conference.

The teacher maintains in the child's assessment notebook or in his/her assessment record what the child is saying in phrases, not sentences. Just enough is recorded to indicate whether the child actually understood the story. The teacher also tries to analyze from the retelling why the child can not comprehend a given text. If the child's accuracy rate with the text is below 95 per cent, then the problem is at the word level, but if the accuracy rate for the text is above 95 per cent, the difficulty lies at the text level.

Development of the Reading Comprehension Skills and Strategies of Individual Students

ELL Learners bring to their classrooms different prior knowledge concerns than do their native English language speaking peers. Some of the ELL students have extensive prior knowledge in their native language and can read well on or above their chronological age level in their native language. Other ELL learners come to the United States from cultures where reading was not emphasized or circumstances did not give families native language literacy opportunities. ELL learners who have a positive attitude toward both their first and second language learning are called "crisscrossers," and of course they are a delight for their teachers.

Rigg and Allen (1999) offer the following four principles regarding the literacy development and prior knowledge of ELL-second language learners:

1. In learning a language you learn to do the things you want to do with people who are speaking that language.
2. A second language, like the first, does not develop linearly, but rather globally.
3. Language can develop in rich context.
4. Literacy develops parallel to language, so as speaking and listening for the second language develop, so do writing and reading.

As far as retelling, it needs to be noted that English language learners have the problem of not bringing rich oral English vocabulary to the stories they are decoding. Therefore, often they "sound the stories out" well, but can not explain what they are about, because they do not know what the words mean.

Use of Oral Reading Fluency in Facilitating Comprehension

At some point it is crucial that just as the nervous, novice bike rider finally relaxes and speeds happily off, so too must the early reader integrate graphophonic cues with semantic and structural ones. Before this is done, the oral quality of early reader's has a stilted beat to it, which of course does not promote reading engagement and enjoyment.

The teacher needs to be at his/her most dramatic to model for children the beauties of voice and nuance that are contained in the texts whose print they are tracking so anxiously. Children love nothing more than to mimic their teacher and can do so legitimately and without hesitation, if the teacher takes time each day to recite a poem with them. The poem might be posted on chart paper and be up on the wall for a week.

First the teacher can model the fluent and expressive reading of this poem. Then with a pointer, the class can recite it with the teacher. As the week progresses, the class can recite it on their own.

Use of Writing Activities to Promote Literary Response and Analysis

In addition to the activities already mentioned, the activities below will promote literary response and analysis:
* Have children take a particular passage from a story and retell it from another character's perspective.

- Challenge children to suggest a sequel or a prequel to any given story they have read.

- Ask the children to recast a story in which the key characters are male into one where the key characters are female (or vice versa). Have them explain how these changes alter the narrative, plot, or outcome.

- Encourage the children to transform a story or book into a Reader's Theater format and record it complete with sound effects for the audio-cassette center of the classroom.

- Have the children produce a newspaper as the characters of a given story would have reported the news in their community.

- Transform the story into a ballad poem or a picture book version for younger peers.

- Give ELL children an opportunity to translate stories into their native language or to author in English with a buddy a favorite story that was originally published in their native language.

"Reading has a central goal, building meaning, that recurs from one situation to the next... Teachers would be better off to regard their role as journeymen readers working with knowledge and purposeful apprentices rather than purveyors of truth."
P.D. Pearson

Skill 2.7   Understand how to apply reading comprehension skills and strategies to informational/expository texts.

Knowledge of Levels of Reading Comprehension (Literal, Inferential, and Evaluative) and Strategies for Promoting Comprehension of Informational/expository Texts at All Three Levels

There are five key strategies for child reading of informational/expository texts.

1. Inferencing is a process that involves the reader making a reasonable judgment based on the information given and engages children to literally construct meaning. In order to develop and enhance this key skill in children, they might have a mini lesson where the teacher demonstrates this by reading an expository book aloud (i.e. one on skyscrapers for young children) and then demonstrates for them the following reading habits: looking for clues, reflecting on what the reader already knows about the topic, and using the clues to figure out what the author means/intends.

2. Identifying main ideas in an expository text can be improved when the children have an explicit strategy for identifying important information. They can make this strategy part of their everyday reading style, "walking" through the following exercises during guided reading sessions. The child should read the passage so that the topic is readily identifiable to him or her. It will be what most of the information is about.

   Next the child should be asked to be on the lookout for a sentence within the expository passage that summarizes the key information in the paragraph. Then the child should read the rest of the passage or excerpt in light of this information and also note which information in the paragraph is less important. The important information the child has identified in the paragraph can be used to formulate the author's main idea. The child reader may even want to use some of the author's own language in stating that idea.

3. Monitoring means self-clarifying: As one reads, the reader often realizes that what he or she is reading is not making sense. The reader then has to have a plan for making sensible meaning out of the excerpt. Cooper and other balanced literacy advocates have a stop and think strategy which they use with children. The child reflects, "Does this make sense to me?" When the child concludes that it does not, the child then either re-reads, reads ahead in the text, looks up unknown words or asks for help from the teacher.

   What is important about monitoring is that some readers ask these questions and try these approaches without ever being explicitly taught them in school by a teacher.

However, these strategies need to be explicitly modeled and practiced under the guidance of the teacher by most, if not all child readers.

4. Summarizing engages the reader in pulling together into a cohesive whole the essential bits of information within a longer passage or excerpt of text. Children can be taught to summarize informational or expository text by following these guidelines. First they should look at the topic sentence of the paragraph or the text and ignore the trivia. Then they should search for information which has been mentioned more than once and make sure it is included only once in their summary. Find related ideas or items and group them under a unifying heading. Search for and identify a main idea sentence. Finally, put the summary together using all these guidelines.

Generating questions can motivate and enhance children's comprehension of reading in that they are actively involved. The following guidelines will help children generate meaningful questions that will trigger constructive reading of expository texts. First children should preview the text by reading the titles and subheadings. Then they should also look at the illustrations and the pictures. Finally they should read the first paragraph. These first previews should yield an impressive batch of specific questions.

Next, children should get into a Dr. Seuss mode and ask themselves a "THINK" question. Make certain that the children write down the question. Then have them read to find important information to answer their "think" question. Ask that they write down the answer they found and copy the sentence or sentences where they found the answer. Also have the students consider whether, in light of their further reading through the text, their original question was a good one or not.

Ask them to be prepared to explain why their original question was a good one or not. Once the children have answered their original "think" question, have them generate additional ones and then find their answers and judge whether these questions were "good" ones in light of the text.

Strategies for Identifying Point of View, Distinguishing Facts from Opinions and Detecting Faulty Reasoning in Informational/expository Texts

Expository texts are full of information which may or may not be factual and which may reflect the bias of the editor or author. Children need to learn that expository texts are organized around main ideas. Expository content is commonly found in newspapers, magazines, content textbooks, and informational reference books (i.e. atlas, almanac, yearbook of an encyclopedia).

The five types of expository texts (also called "text structures") to which the children should be introduced through modeled reading and a teacher facilitated walk through are:

Description text: This usually gives the characteristics or qualities of a particular topic. It can be depended upon to be factual. Within this type of text, the child reader has to use all of his or her basic reading strategies, because these types of expository texts do not have explicit clue words.

Causation or Cause- Effect text: This text is one where faulty reasoning may come into play and the child reader has to use inferential and self-questioning skills to assess whether the stated cause-effect relationship is a valid one. Clue words to look for are: "therefore", "the reasons for", "as a result of", "because", "in consequence of", and "since." The reader must then decide whether the relationship is valid. For example, does the ventricle pump blood into the heart?

Comparison text: This is an expository text which gives contrasts and similarities between two or more objects and ideas. Many social studies, art, and science text books in class and non-fiction books include this contrast. Key words to look out for are: like, unlike, resemble, different, different from, similar to, in contrast with, in comparison to, and in a different vein. It is important that as children examine texts which are talking about illustrated or photographed entities can review the graphic representations for clues to support or contradict the text.

Collection text: This text presents ideas in a group. The writer presents a set of related points or ideas. This text structure is also called a listing or a sequence. The author frequently uses clue words such as first, second, third, finally, and next to alert the reader to the sequence. Based on how well the writer structures the sequence of points or ideas, the reader should be able to make connections. It is important the writer make clear in the expository text how the items are related and why they follow in that given sequence.

Response structure expository texts present a question or response followed by an answer or a solution. Of course, entire mathematics text books and some science and social studies text books are filled with these types of structures. Again it is important to walk the child reader through the excerpt and to sensitize the child to the clue words which signal this type of structure. These words include, but are not limited to the problem is, the question is, you need to solve for, one probable solution would be, an intervention could be, the concern is, and another way to solve this would be.

Use of Reading Strategies for Different Texts and Strategies

As children progress to the older grades (3-6), it is important for the teacher to model for them that in research on a social studies or science exploration, it may not be necessary to read every single word of a given expository information text. For instance, if the child is trying to find out about hieroglyphics, he or she might only read through those sections of a book on Egyptian or Sumerian civilization which dealt with picture writing. The teacher, assisted by a child, should model how to go through the table of contents and the index of the book to identify only those pages which deal with picture writing. In addition other children should come to the front of the room or to the center of the area where the reading group is meeting. They should then, with the support of the teacher, skim through the book for illustrations or diagrams of picture writing which is the focus of their need.

Children can practice the skills of skimming texts and scanning for particular topics that connect with their grade Social Studies, Science and Mathematics content area interests.

Use of Comprehension Skills Before, After, and During Reading

Cooper (2004) advocates that the child ask himself or herself what a text is about before he or she reads it and even during reading of the text, what the text is going to be about. The child should be continually questioning himself or herself as to whether the text confirmed the child's predictions. Of course after completing the text, the child can then review the predictions and verify whether they were correct.

Using another strategy, the child reader looks over the expository text subheadings, illustrations, captions and indices to get an idea about the book. Then the child, still before reading the text, decides whether he or she can find the answer to his or her question.

Use of Oral Language Activities to Promote Comprehension

Taberski advocates using the "Stopping to Think About" strategy with expository texts as well as fictional ones.

This strategy is centered on the reader's using three "steps" as he or she goes through the expository text. These steps may be expressed as questions.

1. What do I, the reader, think is going to happen?
2. What clues in the text or illustrations or graphics lead me to think that this is going to happen?
3. How can I prove that I am right by going back to the text to demonstrate that this does happen or is suggested by actual clues in the text?

Taberski (2000) deliberately uses expository texts that relate to her grade's social studies and science lessons to model for children how to "stop and think" about the way an expository text is organized. She sometimes deliberately reads a section of a text or a non-fiction book aloud until the end of its chapter, so that the children can consider what they have learned about the topic and how it is organized. Then together as a whole class or as a whole guided reading group, they make predictions about what is coming next.

The Role of Oral Language Fluency in Facilitating the Comprehension of Informational/expository Texts

Children on the middle and secondary levels of education, who are studying social studies content, have been exposed to what social studies educators call re-enactments. This is a Reader's Theater-version of history and cultural study based completely on fact and established historical texts and documents.

Even young children will enjoy and gain tremendous additional expository comprehension facility when they are asked to dramatize a well known historical document or song. They may act out the preamble to the Constitution or read aloud as a chorus the Declaration of Independence or dramatize the Battle Hymn of the Republic. This gives children an opportunity to examine in deep form the vocabulary, syntactic, and semantic clues of these texts. They then have to use their oral instruments (voices) to express the appropriate expression for the texts.

If the children are in grades 4 and above, they can also be asked to "explain" in writing how they used the word, syntactic and semantic clues to interpret their oral language recitation. Recitation and writing can be a powerful experience for children grades 4 and up as they build their expository reading and writing skills.

Use of Writing Activities to Promote Comprehension

Use of Text Features (e.g. Index, Glossary) - Graphic Features (e.g. Charts, Maps) and Reference Materials

Traditionally, the aspects of expository text reading comprehension have been taught in a dry format using reference books from the school or public library, particularly, the Atlas, Almanac, and dusty large geography volumes, to teach these necessary and meaningful skills.

Although these worthy library and perhaps classroom library books can still be used, it is much easier to take a simple newspaper to introduce and provide children with daily ongoing, authentic experiences in learning these necessary skills as they also keep up with real world events that affect their daily lives.

Ability to Apply Reading Skills for Various Purposes

What is really intriguing about the use of newspapers as a model and an authentic platform for introducing children into recognizing and using expository text structures, features and references, is that the children can demonstrate their mastery of these structures by putting out their own newspapers detailing their school universe using some of these text structures.

They can also create their own timelines for projects or research papers they have done in class using newspaper models.

Development of Reading Comprehension Skills and Strategies of Individual Students

Both English Language Learners and struggling readers can benefit from the structure and format of the K-W-L approach. It allows them to share their prior experiences and knowledge of the topics covered in the expository text through natural conversation. It provides them with a natural device for the teacher or tutor to customize and to scaffold instruction to meet their linguistic and experiential backgrounds. Through the discussion and sharing of other children's comments, struggling readers and children from ELL backgrounds have an opportunity to learn how to use questions to "walk through" and take notes on expository writing.

Highly proficient readers can do a comparative expository news event study between print accounts, e-news reportage, and broadcast media coverage. They can prepare charts and their own news mock-up to show the similarities and contrasts between what aspects of the event get covered in what media format. They may also want to write to actual reporters and editors from the different media to share their insights and see if these professionals are willing to respond.

"If we want children to become strategic readers, then we create classrooms that reinforce the strategies we've demonstrated and allow children to practice on books that match their needs."
Sharon Taberski

COMPETENCY 3.0 READING ASSESSMENT AND INSTRUCTION

Skill 3.8   Understand Formal and Informal Methods for Assessing Reading Development

The Use of Data and Ongoing Reading Assessment to Adjust Instruction to Meet Students' Reading Needs

Assessment is the practice of collecting information about children's progress, and evaluation is the process of judging the children's responses to determine how well they are achieving particular goals or demonstrating reading skills.

Assessment and evaluation are intricately connected in the literacy classroom. Assessment is necessary because teachers need ways to determine what students are learning and how they are progressing. In addition, assessment can be a tool which can also help students take ownership of their own learning and become partners in their ongoing development as readers and writers. In this day of public accountability, clear, definite and reliable assessment creates confidence in public education.

There are two broad categories of assessment. Informal assessment utilizes observations and other non-standardized procedures to compile anecdotal and observation data/evidence of children's progress. It includes but is not limited to checklists, observations, and performance tasks. Informal assessments are most useful for the information they provide about individual students. The teacher administers informal assessments and can use the results for diagnosis and curriculum planning for specific children. Formal assessment is composed of standardized tests and procedures carried out under circumscribed conditions. Formal Assessments include state tests, standardized achievement tests, NAEP tests, and the like. These scores are usually aggregated, that is, reported as a group, to show the public how a school district or state is doing, usually in comparison with another similar entity.

To be effective, assessment should have the following characteristics:

1. It should be an ongoing process with the teacher making informal or formal assessments on an ongoing basis. The assessment should be a natural part of the instruction and not intrusive.

2. The most effective assessment is integrated into ongoing instruction. Throughout the teaching and learning day, the child's written, spoken and reading contributions to the class or lack thereof, need to and can be continually noted.

3. Assessment should reflect the child's actual reading and writing experiences. The child should be able to show that he or she can read and explain or react to a similar literary or expository work.

4. Assessment needs to be a collaborative and reflective process. Teachers can learn from what the children reveal about their own individual assessments. Children, even as early as grade two, should be supported by their teacher to continually and routinely ask themselves questions assessing their reading. They might ask: "Am I understanding what the author wanted to say?" "What can I do to improve my reading?" and "How can I use what I have read to learn more about this topic?"

    Teachers need to be informed by their own professional observation AND by children's comments as they assess and customize instruction for children.

5. Quality assessment is multidimensional and may include but not be limited to samples of writings, student retellings, running records, anecdotal teacher observations, self-evaluations, and records of independent reading. From this multidimensional data, the teacher can derive a consistent level of performance and design additional instruction that will enhance the child's reading performance.

6. Assessment must take into account children's age and ethnic/cultural patterns of learning.

7. Assess to teach children from their strengths, not their weaknesses. Find out what reading behaviors children demonstrate well and then design instruction to support those behaviors.

8. Assessment should be part of children's learning process and not done TO them, but rather done WITH them.

Characteristics and Uses of Criterion-referenced and Norm-referenced Tests to Assess Reading Development and Identify Reading Difficulties

Criterion-referenced – tests where the children are measured against criteria or guidelines which are uniform for all the test takers. Therefore by definition, no special questions, formats or considerations are made for the test taker who is either from a different linguistic/cultural background or is already identified as a struggling reader/writer. On a criterion-referenced test, it is possible that a child test taker can score 100% because the child may have actually been exposed to all of the concepts taught and mastered them. A child's score on such a test would indicate which of the concepts have already been taught and what he or she needs additional review or support to master.

Two criterion-referenced tests that are commonly used to assess children's reading achievement are the Diagnostic Indicators of Basic Early Literacy Skills (DIBELS) and the Stanford Achievement Test. DIBELS measures progress in literacy from kindergarten to grade three. It can be downloaded from the Internet free at dibels.uoregon.edu. The Stanford is designed to measure individual children's achievement in key school subjects. Subtests covering various reading skills are part of this test. Both DIBELS and the Stanford Achievement Test are group-administered.

DEGREES OF READING POWER (DRP) –This test is targeted to assess how well children understand the meaning of written text in real life situations.
This test is supposed to measure the process of children's reading, not the products of reading such as identifying the main idea and author's purpose.

CTPIII- This is a criterion-referenced test which measures verbal and quantitative ability in grades 3-12. It is targeted to help differentiate among the most capable students, i.e., those who rank above the 80th percentile on other standardized tests. This is a test that emphasizes higher order thinking skills and process-related reading comprehension questions.

Norm-referenced –test in which the children are measured against one another. Scores on this test are reported in percentiles. Each percentile indicates the percent of the testing population whose scores were lower than or the same as a particular child's score. Percentile is defined as a score on a scale of 100 showing the percentage of a distribution that is equal to it or below it. This type of state standardized norm-referenced test is being used in most districts today in response to the No Child Left Behind Act. While this type of test does not help tract the individual reader's progress in his/her ongoing reading development, it does permit comparisons across groups.

There are many more standardized norm-referenced tests to assess children's reading than there are criterion-referenced. In these tests, scores are based on how well a child does compared to others, usually on the local, state and national level. IF the norming groups on the tests are reflective of the children being tested (e.g. same spread of minority, low income, gifted students), the results are more trustworthy.

One of the best known norm-referenced test is the Iowa Test of Basic Skills. It assesses student achievement in various school subjects and has several subtests in reading. Other examples of norm-referenced tests used around the country are the Metropolitan Achievement Tests, the Terra Nova-2, and the Stanford Diagnostic Reading Test-4. These are all group tests. An individual test that reading specialists use with students is the Woodcock Reading Mastery Test.

Concepts of Validity, Reliability, and Bias in Testing

Validity is how well a test measures what it is supposed to measure. Teacher made tests are therefore not generally extremely valid, although they may be an appropriate measure for the validity of the concept the teacher wants to assess for his/her own children's achievement.

Reliability is the consistency of the test. This is measured by whether the test will indicate the same score for the child who takes it more than once.

Bias in testing occurs when the information within the test or the information required to respond to a multiple choice question or constructed response (essay question on the test) is information that is not available to some test takers who come from a different cultural, ethnic, linguistic or socio-economic background than do the majority of the test takers. Since they have not had the same prior linguistic, social or cultural experiences that the majority of test takers have had, these test takers are at a disadvantage in taking the test and no matter what their actual mastery of the material taught by the teacher, can not address the "biased" questions. Generally other "non-biased" questions are given to them and eventually the biased questions are removed from the examination.

To solidify what might be abstract to the reader, on a recent reading test in my school system, the grade four reading comprehension multiple choice had some questions about the well known fairy tale of the gingerbread boy. These questions were simple and accessible for most of the children in the class. But two children who were recent new arrivals from the Dominican Republic had learned English there. They were reading on grade four level, but in their Dominican grade school, the story of the Gingerbread Boy was not a major one. Therefore a question about this story on the standardized reading test did demonstrate examiner bias and was not fair to these test takers.

Scores on a standardized test are often reported in quartiles. This means that the score percentiles have been divided into four parts, called quartiles. This allows the teacher to see at a glance whether a score resides in a high, medium high, medium low, or low region in comparison to other scores.

The Characteristics and Uses of Formal and Informal Assessments

Informal Assessments

A running record of children's oral reading progress in the early grades K-3 is a pivotal informal assessment. It supports the teacher in deciding whether a book a child is reading is matched to his/her stage of reading development. In addition this assessment allows the teacher to analyze a child's miscues to see which cueing systems and strategies the child uses and to determine which other systems the child might use more effectively. Finally the running record offers a graphic account of a child's oral reading.

Generally, a teacher should maintain an annotated class notebook with pages set aside for all the children or individual notebooks for each child. One of the benefits of using running records as an informal assessment is that they can be used with any text and can serve as a tool for teaching, rather than an instrument to report on children's status in class.

Another good point about using running records is that they can be taken repeatedly and frequently by the teacher, so that the educator can truly observe a pattern of errors. This in turn provides the educator with sufficient information to analyze the child's reading over time. As any mathematician or scientist knows, the more samples of a process you gather over time, the more likely the teacher is to get an accurate picture of the child's reading needs.

Using the notations which Marie Clay developed and shared in her *An Observation Study of Early Literacy Achievement*, Sharon Taberski offers in her book, *On Solid Ground*, a lengthy walk through keeping a running record of children's reading. She writes in the child's miscue on the top line of her running record above the text word. Indeed she records all of the child's miscue attempts on the line above the text word. Sharon advises the teacher to make all the miscue notations as the child reads, since this allows the teacher to get additional information about how and why the child makes miscue choices. Additionally, the teacher should note, self corrections (coded SC) when the child is monitoring his/her own reading, crosschecks information, and uses additional information.

As part of the informal assessment of primary grade reading, it is important to record the child's word insertions, omissions, requests for help, and attempts to get the word. In informal assessment the rate of accuracy can be estimated by dividing the child's errors by the total words read.

Results of a running record assessment can be used to select the best setting for the child's reading. If a child reads from 95%-100% correct, the child is ready for independent reading. If the child reads from 92% to 97% right, the child is ready for guided reading. Below 92% the child needs a read-aloud or shared reading activity. Note that these percentages are slightly different from those one would use to match books to readers.

One of the increasingly popular and meaningful forms of informal assessment is the compilation of the literacy portfolio. What is particularly compelling about this type of informal portfolio is that artists, television directors, authors, architects and photographers use portfolios in their careers and jobs. This is a most authentic format for documenting children's literacy growth over time. The portfolio is not only a significant professional informal assessment tool for the teacher, but a vehicle and format for the child reader to take ownership of his or her progress over time. It models a way of compiling one's reading and writing products as a lifelong learner, which is the ultimate goal of reading instruction.

Portfolios can include the following six categories of materials:

Work samples: These can include children's story maps, webs, K-W-L charts, pictures, illustrations, storyboards, and writings about the stories which they have read.

Records of independent Reading and Writing: These can include the children's journals, notebooks or logs of books read with the names of the authors, titles of the books, date completed, and pieces related to books completed or in progress.

Checklists and Surveys: These include checklists designed by the teacher for reading development, writing development, ownership checklists, and general interest surveys.

Self Evaluation Forms: These are the children's own evaluations of their reading and writing process framed in their own words. They can be simple templates with starting sentences such as: "I am really proud of the way I ...

I feel one of my strengths as a reader is _____

To improve the way I read aloud I need to _____

To improve my reading I should _____

Generally at the beginning of a child's portfolio in grade 3 or above there is a letter to the reader explaining the work that will be found in the portfolio and from fourth grade level up, children write a brief reflection detailing their feelings and judgments about their growth as readers and writers.

When teachers are maintaining the portfolios for mandated school administrative review, district review, or even for their own research, they often prepare portfolio summary sheets. These provide identifying data on the children and then a timeline of their review of the portfolio contents plus professional comments on the extent to which the portfolio documents satisfactory and ongoing growth in reading.

Portfolios can be used beneficially for child-teacher and of course, parent/teacher conversations to review the child's progress, discuss areas of strength, set future goals, make plans for future learning activities and evaluate what should remain in the portfolio and what needs to be cleared out for new materials.

Rubrics

Holistic scoring involves assessing a child's ability to construct meaning through writing. It uses a scale called a RUBRIC which can range from 0 to 4.

0- This indicates the piece can not be scored. It does not respond to the topic or is illegible.

1- The writing does respond to the topic, but does not cover it accurately.

2- This piece of writing does respond to the topic but lacks sufficient details or elaboration.

3- This piece fulfills the purpose of the writing assignment and has sufficient development (which refers to details, examples, and elaboration of ideas).

4- This response has the most details, best organization, and presents a well expressed reaction to the original writer's piece.

MISCUE ANALYSIS

This is a procedure that allows the teacher a look at the reading process. By definition, the miscue is an oral response different from the text being read. Sometimes miscues are also called unexpected responses or errors. By studying a student's miscues from an oral reading sample, the teacher can determine which cues and strategies the student is correctly using or not using in constructing meaning. Of course, the teacher can customize instruction to meet the needs of this particular student.

INFORMAL READING INVENTORIES (IRI)

These are a series of samples of texts prearranged in stages of increasing difficulty. Listening to children read through these inventories, the teacher can pinpoint their skill level and the additional concepts they need to work on.

Techniques for Assessing Particular Reading Skills

Sharon Taberski recommends that the teacher build in one-on-one time for supporting individual children as needed in considering what makes sense, sounds right and matches the letters.

She has noted that emergent and early readers tend to focus on meaning without adequate attention to graphophonic cues. She suggests using the following prompts for children who are having problems with graphophonic cues:

Does what you said match the letters?

If the word were what you said ___, what would it have to start with?
Look carefully at the first letters... then look at the middle letters.... then look at the last letters. What could it be?

If it were ____, what would it end with?
Oral retellings can be used to test children's comprehension.

Children who are retelling a story to be tested for comprehension should be told that that is the purpose when they sit down with the teacher.
It is a good idea to let the child start the retelling on his or her own, because then the teacher can see whether he or she needs prompts to retell the story. Many times more

experienced readers summarize what they have read. This summary usually flows out along with the characters, the problem of the story and other details. Other signs that children understand what they are reading when they give an oral retelling include their use of illustrations to support the retelling, references to the exact text in the retelling, emotional reaction to the text, making connections between the text and other stories or experiences they the readers have had, and giving information about the text without the teacher's asking for it.

Awareness of Text Leveling

The classroom library in the context of the balanced literacy approach to reading instruction is focused on leveled books. These are books which have been leveled with the support of Fountas and Pinnell's Guided Reading: *Good First Teaching for All Children* and *Matching Books to Readers: Using Leveled Reading in Guided Reading, K-3*.

The books which are leveled according to the designations in these reference books need to be stored in bins or crates with front covers facing out. This makes them much easier for the children to identify. In that way the children can go through the appropriate levels and find those books that they are particularly interested in which are also at the right level for them to read. These are those books which the children can read with the right degree of reading accuracy. When young children can see the cover of a book, they are more likely to flip through the book until they can independently identify an appealing book. Then they will read a little bit of the book to see if it's "just right." "Just right" leveled books that children can read on their own need to be available for them to read during independent reading. The goal is for the more fluent readers to select books on their own. Ultimately the use of leveled books helps the children, in addition to the teacher, decide which books are "good" or "just right" for them.

Levels are indicated by means of blue, yellow, red, and green dot stickers at their right upper corners which parallel emergent, early, transitional, and fluent reading stages. They are then kept in containers with other "blue," "yellow," "red," and "green" books.

Other lists and resources other than Fountas and Pinnell which can be used to match children with "just right" books include the Reading Recovery level list. Ultimately, the teacher has to individualize whatever leveling is used in the library to address the individual child learners' needs.

Awareness of the Challenges and Supports in a Text

Illustrations can be key supports for emergent and early readers. Teachers should not only use wordless stories (books which tell their narratives through pictures alone), but can also make targeted use of Big Books for read-alouds, so that young children become habituated to the use of illustrations as an important component for constructing meaning. The teacher should model for the child how to reference an illustration for help in identifying a word in the text the child does not recognize. Of course, children can also go on a picture walk with the teacher as part of a mini-lesson or guided reading and anticipate the story (narrative) using the pictures alone to construct meaning.

Decodability: Use literature which contains examples of letter sound correspondences you wish to teach. First, read the literature with the children or read it aloud to them. Then take a specific example from the text and have the children reread it as the teacher points out the letter-sound correspondence to the children. Then ask the children to go through the now familiar literature to find other letter-sound correspondences. Once the children have correctly made the letter-sound correspondences, have them share similar correspondences they find in other works of literature.

Cooper (2004) suggests that children can become word detectives so that they can independently and fluently decode on their own. The child should learn the following word detective routines so that he or she can function as an independent fluent reader who can decode words on his/her own. First the child should read to the end of a sentence. Then the child should search for word parts which he or she knows. The child should also try to decode the word from the letter sounds. As a last resort, the child should ask someone for help or look up the word in the dictionary.

Techniques for Determining Students' Independent, Instructional and Frustration Reading Levels

Instructional reading is generally judged to be at the 95 percent accuracy level, although, Taberski places it at between 92 and 97 percent. Taberski tries to enhance the independent reading levels by making sure that readers on the instructional reading levels read a variety of genres, and have a range of available and interesting books within a particular genre to read.

Taberski's availability for reading conferences helps her to both assess first hand her children's frustration levels and to model ongoing teacher/reader book conversations by scheduling child-initiated reading conferences when she personally replenishes their book bags.

In order to allay children's frustration levels in their reading and to foster their independent reading, it is important to some children that the teacher personally take time out to hear them read aloud and to check for fluency and expression. Children's frustration level can be immeasurably lessened if they are explicitly told by the teacher after they have read aloud that they need to read without pointing and that they should try chunking words into phrases which mimic their natural speech.

Assessment of the Reading Development of Individual Students

For young readers who are from ELL backgrounds, even if they have been born in the United States, the use of pictures validates their story authoring and story telling skills and provides them with access and equity to the literary discussion and book talk of their native English speaking peers. These children can also demonstrate their storytelling abilities by drawing sequels or prequels to the story detailed in the illustrations alone.

They might even be given the opportunity to share the story aloud in their native language or to comment on the illustrations in their native language.

Since many stories today are recorded in two or even three languages at once, discussing story events or analyzing pictures in a different native language is a beneficial practice which can be accomplished in the 21st century marketplace.

Use of pictures and illustrations can also help the K-3 educator assess the capabilities of children who are struggling readers if the children's learning strength is spatial. Through targeted questions about how the pictures would change if different plot twists occurred or how the child might transform the story through changing the illustrations, the teacher can begin to assess struggling reader's deficits and strengths.

Children from ELL backgrounds can benefit from listening to a recorded version of a particular story which they can read along with the tape. This gives them another opportunity to "hear" the story correctly pronounced and presented and to begin to internalize its language structures. In the absence of taped versions of some key stories or texts, the teacher may want to make sound recordings her or himself.

Highly proficient readers can also be involved in creating these literature recordings for use with ELL peers or younger peers. This of course develops oral language proficiency and also introduces these skilled readers into the intricacies of supporting ELL reading instruction. When they actually see their tapes being used by children, they will be tremendously gratified.

"Much of our teaching energy is spent on compensating for an unfavorable environment. It would be far more sensible to use our energies first on the environment itself."
Don Holdaway

Skill 3.9   Understand Multiple Approaches to Reading Instruction

Knowledge of the Significant Theories, Approaches, Practices and Programs for Developing Reading Skills and Reading Comprehension

Decoding

In the late 1960's and the 1970's, many reading specialists, most prominently Fries (1962), believed that successful decoding resulted in reading comprehension. This meant that if children could sound out the words, they would then automatically be able to comprehend the words. Many teachers of reading and many reading texts still subscribe to this theory.

Asking questions

Another theory or approach to the teaching of reading that gained currency in the late sixties and the early seventies was the importance of asking inferential and critical thinking questions of the reader which would challenge and engage the children in the text. This approach to reading went beyond the literal level of what was stated in the text to an inferential level of using text clues to make predictions and to a critical level of involving the child in evaluating the text. While asking engaging and thought-provoking questions is still viewed as part of the teaching of reading, it is only viewed currently as a component of the teaching of reading.

Comprehension "Skills"

As various reading theories, practices, and approaches percolated during the 1970's and 1980's, many educators and researchers in the field came to believe that the teacher of reading had to teach a set of discrete "Comprehension Skills" (Otto et al, 1977). Therefore the reading teacher became the teacher of each individual comprehension skill. Children in such classrooms came away with: main idea, sequence, cause and effect, and other concepts that were supposed to make them better comprehenders. However, did it make them lifelong readers?

Transactional Approach

During the late 1970's and early 1980's, researchers in the field of education, psychology and linguistics, began to examine how the reader comprehends. Among them was Louise Rosenblatt who posited that reading is a transaction between the reader and the text. It is Rosenblatt (1978) who explained successful reading as the reader constructing a meaning from the text that reflected both the reader and the text. She described two general purposes for reading: *efferent* and *aesthetic*. Efferent reading is looking for and remembering information to use functionally. Examples would be filling out a job application, reading a story in preparation for a test, or reading a newspaper article to find out who won the state basketball championship. Aesthetic reading is done to connect one's own life to the text, to be swept away by the beauty of a poem, or to respond emotionally to a book such as *Bridge to Terabithia*.

These differing purposes call for somewhat different reading strategies: one might skim the newspaper article for basketball information but read a poem closely ten times and create mental images of different passages. Lastly, when children are asked to read all fiction efferently (What's the setting? What's the main conflict in the plot? There will be a test on this on Thursday!), it can thwart a child's joy in the written word and work against the student's desire to be a lifelong reader.

Bottom-up, Top-down, Interactional Theories of Reading

Bottom-up theories of reading assume that children learn from part-to-whole starting with the smallest segments possible. Instruction begins with a strong phonics approach, learning letter-sound relationships and often using basal readers or *decodable books*. Decodable books are vocabulary-controlled using language from word families with high predictability. Thus we get sentences like "Nan has a tan fan." Reading is seen as skills-based, and the skills are taught one at a time.

Top-down theories of reading suggest that reading begins with the reader's knowledge, not the print. Children are seen as having a drive to construct meaning. This stance views reading as moving from the whole to the parts. An early top-down theory was the *whole word* approach. Children memorized high-frequency words to assist them in reading the Dick and Jane books of the 30s. Then teachers helped children discover letter-sound correpondences in what they read. A more recent top-down theory is the *whole language* approach.

This approach was influenced by research on how young children learned language. It was thought that children could learn to read as naturally as they learned to talk. Children were viewed as able to learn to read almost as effortlessly as they learned oral language. The term "emergent literacy" came into vogue as a description of how children engaged in literate behaviors from birth onward.

Whole language advocates also challenged the notion of reading readiness as a set of discrete skills which children needed to learn BEFORE they began reading. Whole language practitioners tried to re-create in their classrooms the same stimulating environment that many children enjoyed in highly literate homes before entering school. Thus, children were surrounded by print in their classrooms, using quality literature often printed in Big Books and were viewed as writers from the start. Hence journals kept by kindergarten children. Advocates of whole language viewed the "skill'em-drill'em-and-kill'em" approach based on bottom-up theories as a deadly dull introduction to the world of reading.

Interactive theories of reading combine the strengths of both bottom-up and top-down approaches. Teachers need to be able to teach decoding, vocabulary, and comprehension skills to support children's drive for meaning and desire for a stimulating exchange with high-quality literary texts from their earliest days in school. Strategies include shared, guided, and independent reading, Big Books, reading and writing workshops, and the like. Today this approach is called the *balanced literacy approach*. It is considered to be a synthesis of the best from bottom-up and top-down methods.

Literacy and Literacy Learning

To be literate in the 21st century world means more than being able to read and write. To live well and happily in today's society an individual has to be able to read, not only newspapers and books, but emails, blogs, directions for how to use one's cell phone, and the like. There has evolved a "disconnect" between the isolated reading comprehension skills the schools were teaching and the literacy skills including listening and speaking that are crucial for employment and personal and academic success. Thornburg (1992, 2003) has also noted that technology capacities and the ability to communicate online are now integral parts of our sense of literacy.

Cooper (2004) views literacy as reading, writing, thinking, listening, viewing, and discussing. These are not viewed as separate activities or components of instruction, but rather as developing and being nurtured simultaneously and interactively. Children learn these abilities by engaging in authentic explorations, readings, projects and experiences.

Just as in learning how to ride a bike, the learner goes through various approximations before learning how to actually ride the bike, so too does the reader with the scaffold (support) of the teacher go through various approximations before developing his/her own independent literacy skills and capacities.

Emergent Literacy: the concept that young children are emerging into reading and writing with no real beginning or ending point. Children are introduced into the word of print as soon as their parents read board books to them at the age of one or two. When children scribble write or use invented spelling during the preschool years, they reveal themselves as detectives of the written word, having watched parents and teachers make lists, write thank-you notes, or leave messages. This view of the reader assumes that all children have a drive to make meaning in print and will begin doing it almost on their own if surrounded by a print-rich environment.

Reading Readiness: an approach which is antithetical to emergent literacy in that it assumes that all children must have mastered a sequence of reading skills <u>before</u> they can begin to read. This approach stands in contrast to emergent literacy.

Language Acquisition: continuous and never-ending. From the perspective of this theory and research, all children come to school with a language base which the school must build on. As a consequence of the connection between oral language and reading, it is important that schools build literacy experiences around the language the child brings to the school.

Prior Knowledge, Schemata, Background, and Comprehension

Schemata are structures which represent generic concepts stored in our memory (Rumelhart, 1980). Young children develop their schemata through experiences. Prior knowledge and the lack of experiences in some cases influence comprehension. The more closely the reader's experiences and schemata approximate those of the writer, the more likely the reader is to comprehend the text. It is obvious that for many children from non-native English language speaking backgrounds and perhaps for those from struggling socio-economic family structures schemata deficits indicate the need for intense teacher support as these children become emergent and early readers.

Often the teacher will have to model and scaffold for the child the steps to form a schemata from the information provided in a text.

Comprehension

Cooper defines comprehension as: "a strategic process by which readers construct or assign meaning to a text by using the clues in the text and their own prior knowledge. " We view comprehension as a process where the reader transacts with the text to construct or assign meaning. Reading and writing are both interconnected and mutually supportive. Comprehension is a strategic process in which readers adjust their reading to suit their reading purpose and the type or genre of text they are reading. Narrative and expository texts require different reading approaches because of their different text structures.

Strategic readers also call into play their metacognitive capacities as they analyze texts so that they are self aware of the skills needed to construct meaning from the text structure.

The Role of Literature in Developing Literacy

The balanced literacy approach advocates the use of "real literature"—recognized works of the best of children's fiction and non-fiction trade books and winners of such awards as the Newberry and Caldecott medals for helping children develop literacy.

Balanced literacy advocates argue that:

- Real literature engages young readers and assures that they will become lifelong readers.

- Real literature also offers readers a language base that can help them expand their expressiveness as readers and as writers.

- Real literature is easier to read and understand than grade-leveled texts

There are districts in the United States where the phonics-only approach is heavily embedded. However, the majority of school districts would describe their approach to reading as the balanced literacy approach which includes phonics work as well as the use of real literature texts. To contrast the phonics and balanced literacy approaches as opposite is inaccurate, since a balanced approach includes both.

It is important to go online and to visit the key resources of the NCTE, National Council of Teachers of English, and the IRA, International Reading Association, to keep abreast of the latest research in the field.

Strategies for Planning, Organizing, Managing, and Differentiating Reading Instruction to Support the Reading Development of All Students

The physical set up of your classroom is exceedingly important to support the effective development of all children. The homey look of the classroom belies its deliberate design as a space where children can experience, practice, share and learn. Some teachers have done away with the large desk and use smaller tables instead. Sharon Taberski advocates for young children K-3 adjusting the height of the table legs so the children can use the tables as writing spaces and sit on the floor. Sharon gives each of her children a personal 12"x 9"x 2" tray on which they place their home possessions, books, homework, folder, etc. This is kept in a small storage unit near the coat closet during the day.

Children put their completed homework in a wire basket and notes from parents or the office in a second wire basket. Supplies such as pencils, markers, crayons, scissors, and erasers are not brought from home, but rather available for all in the class from "community" containers at the center of each of the children's tables.

All the children's reading, writing, and individual math folders are stored together in plastic bins in the meeting area. Every child has an individual book bag which is kept in one of two large wicker baskets set in different areas of the room.

Understanding Our Role and Goals

This storing of materials away from children decreases their "fiddling with" their belongings during class, makes the room look much neater, and frees the children to focus on their learning experiences, rather than where their belongings are at any given time of day.

As you can see on the accompanying diagram the 10'x10' meeting area is the center of classroom learning. This is where the whole class is gathered at the beginning of the reading and the writing workshop and for sharing sessions. It is also the demonstration and modeling center for both the teacher and for children.

Generally, the presenter sits on the adult chair (in some balanced literacy classrooms, this is a rocking chair) near the easel with the chart. Generally, this chair and the easel are strategically positioned so that the teacher can see the door and any visitors or urgent messages from the office. Rearranging furniture during the day takes away from instruction time and is disruptive. Have a designated comfortable section of the room that can be a gathering place for a literacy community and then organize the rest of the classroom activities around that center.

The conference table which is at the back of the room (see diagram) is another key piece of classroom space furniture. It is the place where the four or five children and the teacher confer, wait and do their work. Having children come to a set conference table, rather than the teacher's going to them (although some teachers do advocate going to the children) saves time as far as Taberski is concerned. It serves to keep her and the children on task.

Taberski keeps two separate trays of supplies: a small magnetic board, letters, chalkboard, chalk, sentence strips, index cards, and blank books for her demonstrations during her conferences. She believes that teachers should store materials close to where they are used, so the teacher does not have to take time from the child to get up and get the materials.

The Classroom Library

On the tables, Taberski generally has book crates with books that are not leveled. Children choose from these books during the first independent reading session of her day which is from 8:40-9:00. During the second reading session from 9:30-10:20 the children select books from the leveled reading bins which are stored on the bookcase shelves.

Beyond the leveled books, which have already been discussed, Taberski also maintains a non-leveled, non fiction library which includes dictionaries, atlases, almanacs and informational books related to the themes, projects and investigations that the children will undertake throughout the year.

Beyond the leveled books and non-fiction books in the classroom, Taberski and other balanced literacy advocates generally include at least 10-15 big books which they routinely use to engage children with the text.

Since Guided Reading with groups of 6 children is a major part of the balanced literacy approach, Taberski and other disciplined and dedicated teacher educators "bundle" up six copies of selected books so that they can distribute them to their guided reading groups whenever they choose to do them. Taberski models the concept of a home library collection for the children by keeping books which she particularly likes in a bookcase behind her chair. She sometimes places "her" books on the easel so that they can be shared by the children and returned to her.

Wall Works

Much of creating a family atmosphere lies in the use of the room walls to document the children's learning experiences, skills work, and readings.

Generally at least one wall in a reading classroom is the Chart Wall. Charts with various spelling patterns discussed in class can be posted. If a child later has issues or concerns with that particular pattern, he or she should be directed to look at and to review the chart.

One of the centerpieces of the K-2 classroom is the High Frequency Word Chart. This is a growing list of commonly used words which the teacher tapes under the appropriate beginning letter according to the children's directions. At the end of each month, the newest high frequency words go into the children's folders and become part of their spelling words. Therefore reading, writing, and spelling are all intricately connected. Supplies for children K-3 and beyond can include:

- A red plastic double pocket reading folder
- A blue plastic double pocket reading folder
- A four sectioned pressed board spelling/poetry folder
- A 4" x 6" assessment notebook for reading
- A 4" x 6" assessment notebook for writing
- A reading response notebook (loose-leaf- 60 pages)
- A handwriting notebook

The Reading Folder contains the assessment notebooks, the reading response notebooks, a Weekly Reading Log, and the strategy sheets the child may be using that particular week.

The Assessment Notebook is a key evaluative tool and a recording document for the conscientious balanced literacy specialist. The teacher uses the notebook to record the child's running record, the retellings of stories shared by the child, and summarizing talks about leveled books read. Within the assessment books, the teacher also has notes about the child's progress, the strategies the child has learned to use well, the books he or she has read and those strategies the child still needs to practice. These assessment notebooks must be kept accessible so that the teacher can use them to confer with the child, parents, and administrator as needed. During conferences with parents, the teacher will use information from the assessment notebooks, individual children's running records (for use with individual parents only), children's work samples, and the children's weekly logs, spelling folders, and child-created dictionaries. These authentic examples of children's work will provide a rich picture to parents and grandparents of the rich world of reading in the classroom today.

The reading response notebook becomes a compilation of reading strategy sheets and children's writings and art in response to literature.

The Weekly Reading Log allows the child to maintain for him- or herself the titles of books they have read and written a bit about the narrative, style, and genre of that given book.

Book Bags: These are 10" x 12" heavy duty freezer bags which keep 3-10 books a child is "working on" during his/her free time. The teacher generally matches the children to the books and changes these books as needed by the children.

Writing Folders

Children keep several pieces of writing in their folders at a time. Within the writing folder is also a handwriting notebook and a beginning word book as well. The Spelling/Poetry Folder is one which helps children focus on the sequence of letters in words and learn more how words work.

The balanced literacy advocates have a definite schedule for the teaching of reading and writing workshop from which they generally do not deviate. A sample follows.

8:40-9:00- FIRST INDEPENDENT READING/WORD STUDY GROUP

9:00-9:30- MEETING-WHOLE GROUP SESSION in the meeting area
Read Aloud, Shared Reading, or Shared Writing

9:30-10:30- READING WORKSHOP
Reading Conferences or Guided Reading
Second Independent Reading
Reading Share 10:20-10:30

10:30-10:40- Writing Mini Lesson or Writing Share

10:40-11:20- Writing Workshop Writing Conferences, Guided Writing, Modeled Writing, Independent Writing

(11:10-11:20)-Writing Share

Adjustment of Reading Instruction Based on Ongoing Assessment

The running records taken of children help the teacher learn about the cueing systems that children use. It is important for the teacher to adjust reading instruction based on the pattern of miscues gathered from several successive reading records. When the teacher carefully reviews a given student's substitutions and self corrections, certain patterns begin to surface. A child may use visual cues as he or she reads and adds meaning to self correct. To the alert teacher, the reliance on visual miscues indicates that the reader doesn't make sense of what she is reading. This means that the teacher needs to check to see what cueing system the child uses when he or she is reading "just right" books. Children, who use meaning and structure but not visual/graphophonic cues, need to be reminded and facilitated to understand the importance of getting and reconstructing the author's message. They have to be able to share the author's story, not their own.

Not only can and should the teacher use the material in the children's ongoing assessment notebook to adjust the child's current instruction but the material also serves to document for the child his/her growth as a successful reader over time. In addition, if the same concerns surface over the use of a particular cueing system or high frequency word, the teacher can adjust the class wall chart and even devote a whole class lesson to the particular element.

Instructional Reading Strategies for Promoting the Development of Particular Reading Skills

Phonemic awareness can be developed through using leveled books that deal with rhyming words and segmenting phonemes into words. Children can also work with word or letter strips to continue the poems from the books and create their own "sequels" to the phoneme-filled story. They can also create an in-style rhyming story using some of the same phonemes from the leveled story they have heard.

Word Identification- Selective Cue Stage. Sometimes children have not yet experienced an awareness of the conventions of print and labeling in their own home environments. The teacher or an aide may have to go on a label adventure and support children in recognizing or affixing labels to parts of the classroom, halls and school building. A neighborhood walk with a digital or hand held camera may be required to help children identify uses and functions of print in society. A classroom photo essay or bulletin board could be the outgrowth of such an activity.

Sight Vocabulary- Beginning readers may enjoy outdoing Dolch (1936), who compiled the best known sight vocabulary word list. They can create their own class version of this list with illustrations and even some comments about why they have nominated certain words for the list.

Uses of Large Group, Small Group, and Individualized Reading Instruction

The framework for organizing the balanced literacy classroom is referred to as the one book-whole class mode. What this means is that everyone in the class has experiences with the same book. Everyone in the class discusses the literature. The teacher starts by activating prior knowledge and developing the context or background for the piece of literature. Some of the children within the class may have less prior knowledge or context with which to frame the book. The teacher will need to provide a preview of the book or develop key concepts to provide a stronger base for what the class will read together.

Some children will have to work with a paraprofessional or with a reading tutor before the class studies the book. Different modes of reading are accommodated within the class, by the books being read as a read-aloud, as part of shared reading or as guided reading. Student reader choices can also include: cooperative reading, reading with a partner, or independent reading.

Following the reading, the children respond to it which can be done through a literature circle and/or the whole class or in writing. Based on assessments, the teacher will often form small ability groups for guided reading and mini-lessons. In this situation, the small group of children will all be working on the same skill(s). These ability groups are not permanent but will change as the children's needs change.

Strategies for Selecting and Using Meaningful Reading Materials at Appropriate Levels of Difficulty

Matching young children with "just right" books fosters their reading independently, no matter how young they are. The teacher needs to have an extensive classroom library of books. Books that emergent readers and early readers can be matched with should have fairly large print, appropriate spacing, so that the reader can easily see where word begins and ends, and few words on each page so that the young reader can focus on all important concerns of top-to bottom, left-to-right, directionality, and the one-to-one match of word to print.

Illustrations for young children should support the meaning of the text and language patterns and predictable text structures should make these texts appealing to young readers. Most important of all the content of the story should relate to the children's interests and experiences as the teacher knows them.

Only after all these considerations have been addressed, can the teacher select "just right" books from an already leveled bin or list. In a similar fashion, when the teacher is selecting books for transitional and fluent readers, the following ideas need to be taken into account:

The book should take at least two sittings to read, so children can get used to reading longer books. The fluent and transitional reader needs to deal with more complex characters and more intricate plotting. Look for books that set the stage for plot development with a compelling beginning. Age appropriateness of the concepts, plot and themes is important so that the child will sustain interest in the book. Look for book features such as a list of chapters to help children navigate through the book.

Series books are wonderful to introduce at this point in the children's development.

Creation of an Environment that Promotes Love of Reading

The aforementioned creation of the meeting area and the reading chair (sometimes a rocking chair) with throw pillows around it promotes a love of reading. Beyond that, some classrooms have adopted an author's hat, decorated with the pictures of famous authors and book characters which children wear when they read from their own works.

Many classrooms also have children's storyboards, artwork, story maps, pop-up books, and "in the style of" writing inspired by specific authors. Some teachers buy calendars for the daily schedule which celebrate children's authors or types of literature. Children are also encouraged to bring in public library books and special books from their home libraries. The teacher can model this habit of sharing beautiful books and inviting stories from his or her home library.

In addition, news stories about children's authors, series books, television versions of books, theatrical film versions of books, stuffed toy book character decorations and other memorabilia related to books can be used to decorate the room.

Various chain book stores including Barnes and Nobles and Borders give out free book marks and promotional display materials related to children's books which can be available in the room for children to use as they read independently or in their guided groups. They might even use these artistic models to inspire their own book themed artifacts.

Strategies for Promoting Independent Reading in the Classroom and at Home

Pre-select books for the children which are just right for them. Provide the children with a quiet, relaxing space within the classroom where they can go to read these books. Don't get upset if they seem to take a break or wander around the room after fifteen minutes. Adults take breaks as well.

Make certain that the children who are reading independently fill in their weekly logs. Beyond telling what books they were reading and how many pages they have read, have the children respond to the following prompts:

This week I was successful at...

Next week I plan to...

A response can also be an illustration or a sentence or two about the book.

Deliberately assign a child or a pair of children to read big books. These are a guaranteed success for the children because they have already been shared in class. Some children enjoy reading these independently using big rulers to point at words. This provides them with a sense of mastery over the words and ownership of their independent reading.

Some children enjoy working on their own strategy sheet such as a story map, character map, or storyboard panel, to demonstrate how they can apply a strategy to their own independent learning.

Uses of Instructional Technology to Promote Reading Development

One of the most interesting ways in which the web complements the Reading and Writing Workshop involves the proliferation of author specific websites. If used judiciously, these web resources allow authors to come into the classroom and allow children to write, question, discuss and share their literacy experiences with the authors themselves. Children can also readily become part of a distanced community of peers who are also reading works by a given author.

For instance, children who have been introduced to the work of Faith Ringgold, the author of *Tar Beach*, can easily visit her online site, www.faithringgold.com. Here they will not only find extensive biographic data on Ringgold, but they will also be able to learn a song inspired by her main character Cassie. They will be able to help illustrate a new story Ringgold has put up on the website, and also see if any of the questions they may have generated in their shared or independent reading of her books, has already been answered in the "frequently asked questions" section of her web resource. A few of the author websites respond online to individual children's questions.

There are even some reader response web resources such as the spaghetti review web site where young readers can post their response to different books they are reading. **http://www.book-club-review.com/view.php?cid=1**

Awareness of Strategies and Resources for Supporting Individual Students

Children who come from family backgrounds where English is not spoken lack a solid understanding of its syntactic structure. Therefore as they are being assessed using the oral running record, they may need additional support from their teacher in examining the structure and meaning of English. A child from a non-native English Language speaking background may often pronounce words that make no sense to him or her and just go on reading. They have to learn to stop to construct meaning. This child may have to be prompted to self-correct.

Children from non-native English Language speaking backgrounds can benefit from independent reading opportunities to listen to a familiar story on tape and read along. This also gives them practice in listening to Standard English oral reading. Often these children can begin to internalize the language structures by listening to the book on tape several times.

Highly proficient readers can sometimes support early readers through a partner relationship. Some children, particularly the emergent and beginning early readers, benefit from reading books with partners. The partners sit side by side and each one takes turns reading the entire text.

Use of talking book and author web resources provides special needs learners with visual or auditory handicapping conditions immediate contact with authors. This can lead to direct sharing in the joy of oral language story telling. In addition to the accessibility of the keyboard, children's responses to literature can be shared with a broad network of other readers, including close and distance peers. Technology literally invites special needs learners into the circle of connected readers and writers.

COMPETENCY 4.0   **INTEGRATION OF KNOWLEDGE AND UNDERSTANDING**

Skill 4.10   **Prepare an organized, developed analysis on a topic related to one or more of the following: foundations of reading development; development of reading comprehension; reading assessment and instruction**

Material that may appear on the open-ended responses will come from Competencies 1 through 3 in this guide. Understanding the material from all three sections will allow you to complete thoroughly written responses to each of the two open-ended response questions on your exam.

Competency 1 - Foundations of Reading Development (Skills 1.1-1.4)

Competency 2 - Development of Reading Comprehension (Skills 2.5-2.7)

Competency 3 - Reading Assessment and Instruction (Skills 3.8-3.9)

Open-ended response questions may have multiple parts to each one. Answers to the open-ended responses should be thorough and should cover each part of the given question. By taking the time to plan out a response through brainstorming and the use of an organizer, a test-taker can get his or her ideas down onto paper before beginning a response.

The open-ended responses are scored by at least two different individuals. It is important that they are each able to read the responses; therefore, hand-writing should be legible, and sentences should be well-thought out. Ensure that your writing flows well and makes sense. Include as many details and examples as possible. Think of your experiences in the classroom thus far. Integrate personal examples when applicable. These will show the scorers that you have an in-depth understanding of the question and are able to meet the questions objective(s).

When you have completed each open-ended response, reread your work. Check for accuracy and that you have answered all parts of the given question. Be sure to monitor your time wisely. Even if you think you might run out of testing time, attempt to complete as much as you can so that earn some points from this portion of the exam.

GLOSSARY

These definitions are critical for success on all multiple choice questions on the examinations. Proper use of these terms, is crucial for success in tackling a constructed response involving balanced literacy.

ABILITY GROUPING- grouping of children with similar needs for instructional purposes. Ability groups do not remain constant throughout the year, but change as the children's needs within them change.

ALLITERATION- occurs when words begin with the same consonant sound, as in *Peter Piper picked a pair of pickled peppers.*

ALPHABETIC PRINCIPLE- the idea that written spellings represent spoken words.

ANCHOR BOOK- a balanced literacy term for a book that is purposely read repeatedly and used as part of both the reading and writing workshop.

It is a good idea to use certain books that become the children's familiar and cherished favorites for both reading and then to inspire children's writing.

ASSONANCE- Occurs when words begin with the same vowel sound.

AUTHENTIC ASSESSMENT- assessment activities which reflect the actual workplace, family community and school curriculum.

BALANCED LITERACY LESSON FORMAT- The Balanced Literacy Approach has its own specific format for the delivery of the literacy lesson, whether it is a reading or writing workshop lesson. The format begins with a 10-15 minute mini-lesson which the teacher delivers to the whole class. This mini-lesson is then followed by a thirty-minute small group (when the children break into small groups to work) lesson. It concludes with a 10-minute share during which the whole class reconvenes to share what they have done in the small groups.

One can refer to this format as the whole-small-whole group approach.

BENCHMARKS- school state, or nationally mandated statements of the expectations for student learning and achievement in various content areas.

BICS-BASIC INTERPERSONAL COMMUNICATION SKILLS (ELL term- Bilingual Education)- learning second language skills and becoming proficient in a second language through face to face interaction-translation through speaking, listening, and viewing.

BLENDING- the process of hearing separate phonemes and being able to merge them together to read the word.

BOOK FEATURES- children need to be familiar with the following book features: front and back cover, title and half- title page, dedication page, table of contents, prologue and epilogue, and foreword and after notes. For factual books, children need to be familiar with: labels, captions, glossary, index, headings and subheadings of chapters, charts and diagrams, and sidebars.

CHECKLIST- an assessment form which lists targeted learning and social behaviors as indicators of achievement, knowledge or skill. They can be professionally- or teacher-prepared.

CINQUAIN- a five line poem that can be read and then used as a model for writing. Generally line 1 of this format is a single word, line 2 has 2 words, which describe the title of line 1, line 3 is comprised of 3 words which are movement words, line 4 has 4 words which express feeling and line 5 has a single word which is a synonym for line 1's single word.

COMPREHENSION- this occurs when the reader correctly interprets the print on the page and constructs meaning from it. Comprehension depends on activating prior knowledge, cultural and social background of the reader, and the reader's ability to use comprehension monitoring strategies.

CONCEPTS ABOUT PRINT- include: how to handle a books, how to look at print, directionality, sequencing, locating skills, punctuation, and concepts of letters and words.

CONSONANT DIAGRAPHS- two consecutive consonants that represent one new speech sound. In the word "digraph" the *ph* which sounds like /f/ is a digraph.

CONTEXTS- sentences deliberately prepared by the teacher which include sufficient contextual clues for the children to decipher meaning.

CONTEXTUAL REDEFINITION- using context to determine word meaning.

COOPERATIVE READING- Children read with a partner or buddy. It can be silent or oral reading.

CRISSCROSSERS- an ELL term for second language learners who have a positive attitude toward both first language and second language learning. These second language learners, children from ELL backgrounds, are comfortable navigating back and forth between the two languages as they learn.

CUES- as they self monitor their reading comprehensions, readers have to integrate various sources of information or cues to help them construct meaning from text and graphic illustrations.

DECODING-"sounding out" a printed sequence of letters based on knowledge of letter sound correspondences.

DIPHTHONGS- two vowels in one syllable where the two sounds are heard. For instance in the word *house* both the "o" and the "u" are heard.

DIRECTIONALITY-children use their fingers to indicate left to right direction and return sweep to the next line.

DIFFERENTIATED INSTRUCTION- The need for the teacher, based on observation of individual student's work, progress, test results, fluency, and other reading/literacy behaviors, to provide modified instruction and alternative strategies or activities. These activities are specifically developed by the teacher to address the individual student's different needs.

EARLY READERS- recognize most high frequency words and many simple words. They use pictures to confirm meaning. Using meaning, syntax, and phonics, they can figure out most simple words. They use spelling patterns to figure out new words. They are gaining control of reading strategies. They use their own experiences and background knowledge to predict meanings.

They occasionally use story language in their writing. This stage follows emergent reading.

EMERGENT READERS- the stage of reading in which the reader understands that print contains a consistent message. The reader can recognize some high frequency words, names, and simple words in context. Pictures can be used to predict meaning. The emergent reader begins to attend to left to right directionality and features of print and may identify some initial sounds and ending sounds in words.

ENCODE- to change a message into symbols. For example, readers encode oral language into writing.

ENGLISH as a SECOND LANGUAGE- a way of teaching English to speakers of other languages using English as the language of instruction.

EXPOSITORY TEXT- is non-fiction that provides information and facts. This text type is what newspapers, science, mathematics and history texts use. Currently there is much focus, even in elementary schools, on teaching children how to comprehend and author expository texts. They must produce brochures, guides, recipes, and procedural accounts on most elementary grade levels. The teaching of reading of expository texts requires working with a particular vocabulary and concept structure that is very different from that of the narrative text. Therefore time must be taken to teach the reading of expository texts and contrast it with the reading of narrative texts.

FIRST LANGUAGE- an ELL term for the language any child acquires in the first few years of life. It is through this acquired language that the child acquires phonological and phonemic awareness.

FLUENT READERS- identify most words automatically. They can read chapter books with good comprehension. They consistently monitor, cross-check, and self-correct reading. They can offer their own interpretations of text based on personal experiences and prior reading experiences. Fluent readers are capable of reading a variety of genres independently. Furthermore, they can respond to texts or stories by sharing pertinent examples from their lives. They can also readily make connections to other books which they have read. Finally, they are capable of beginning to create spoken and written writings which are in the style of a particular author.

FORMAL ASSESSMENT- a test or an observation of a performance task which is done under controlled and regulated conditions.

FUNCTIONAL READING- the reading of instructions, recipes, coupons, classified ads, notices, signs, and other documents which we have to read and correctly interpret in school and in society.

GRADE EQUIVALENT/GRADE SCORE- a score transformed from a raw score on a standardized test into the equivalent score earned by an average student in the norming group.

GRAPHIC ORGANIZERS- graphic organizers express relationships among various ideas in visual form including: sequence, timelines, character traits, fact and opinion, main idea and details, differences and likenesses. Graphic organizers are particularly helpful for visual learners.

GUIDED READING- one of the key modes of instruction in the balanced literacy approach. During guided reading, the teacher "guides" the child through silent reading of a text by giving them prompts, target questions, and even helping the child start an answer to a specific prompt or question. At the end of each guided reading section or excerpt of the text, the child stops to talk with the teacher about the text. By definition, guided reading is an interactive discussion between the child and the teacher. This mode of reading instruction is generally used when children need extra support in constructing meaning because the text is complex or because their current independent reading capacities are still limited.

HIGH FREQUENCY- frequently used words. These words appear many more times than do other words in ordinary reading material. Examples of such words include: *as, in, of,* and *the*. These words are also sometimes called service words. These words are also part of sight vocabulary words. A classic best-known high frequency word list was generated by Dolch (1936).

INDEPENDENT READING- a set period of time within the daily literacy block when children read books with 95%-100% accuracy on their own. This reading of books by themselves which they can understand without teacher support promotes lifelong literacy and love of learning, which enhances reading mileage, builds fluency, and helps children orchestrate integrated cue strategies.

INFORMAL ASSESSMENT- observations of children made under informal conditions; these can include kid watching, checklists, and individual child/teacher conversations.

INFORMAL READING INVENTORY (IRI) - a series of reading excerpts that can be used to determine a child's reading strengths and needs in comprehension and decoding. Many published reading series have an IRI to go with their series.

JUSTIFIED PRINT- the positioning of print on the page so that each line ends at the same margin.

KID WATCHING- term used within the balanced literacy approach for the teacher's deliberate, detailed, and recorded observations of individual student and class literacy behaviors., often done during small group work. The teacher then reconfigures lessons on experiences to meet the students' individual and group needs.

KINESTHETIC- learning is tactile; as contrasted with an activity where the learner sits still or attempts to sit still in one place. Cutting and moving syllable or word strips or using sandpaper letters are kinesthetic activities.

LANGUAGE EXPERIENCE- Children giving dictation to the teacher who writes their words on a chart or their drawings. This shows children that words can be written down.

LEARNING LOGS- daily records of what students have learned.

LISTENING POST- sets of headphones attached to a single tape player. Children can go to centers where they listen to audiotapes of books while reading the print book. These posts are in many libraries as well.

LITERATURE CIRCLES- a group discussion involving four to six children who have read the same work of literature (narrative or expository text). They talk about key parts of the work, relate it to their own experience, listen to the responses of others, and discuss how parts of the text relate to the whole.

MANIPULATION- moving around or switching sounds within a word or words within a phrase or sentence.

MEANING VOCABULARY- words whose meanings children understand and can use.

MISCUE- an oral reading error made by a child which differs from the actual printed text.

MISCUE ANALYSIS- the teacher keeps a detailed recording of the errors or inaccurate attempts of a child reader during a reading assessment. These are recorded within a running record. This helps the teacher see whether the cues-syntactic, semantic, or graphophonemic-the child is using are accurate.

MONITORING READING- various strategies that children use to monitor their readings. A sample are maintaining fluency by bringing prior knowledge to the story to make predictions, using these predictions to do further checking, searching, and self-correcting as the story progresses, and using problem-solving word study skills to make links from known words to unknown words.

MORPHEMES- the smallest units of meaning in words. There are two types of morphemes; free morphemes, which can stand alone such as *love,* and bound morphemes, which must be attached to another morpheme to carry meaning such as *ed* in *loved.*

NARRATIVE TEXT- one of the two basic text structures. The narrative text tells or communicates a story. Narrative texts are novels, short stories and plays. Some poems are narratives as well. The narrative text needs to be taught differently than the expository text because of its structure.

ONE TO ONE MATCHING- matching one spoken word with one written word.

ONSET-RIME BLENDING –ONSET- Everything before the vowel and RIME (the vowel and everything after it). For example, the word "sleep" can be broken into /sl/ and /eep/. Word families are build using rimes. The /eep/ word family would include *jeep, keep* and *weep.*

ORTHOGRAPHY- a method of representing spoken language through letters and diacritics.

PERCENTILE- if a child scores at the 56th percentile for his/grade level, his/her score is equal to or above that of 56 percent of the children taking that standardized test and below that of 46 percent of the children on whose scores the test was normed.

PERFORMANCE ASSESSMENT- having children do a task that demonstrates their knowledge, skills and competency. Having children author their own alphabet book on a particular topic would be a performance assessment for knowledge of the alphabet.

PHONEME- The speech sound units that make a difference in meaning. The word "rope" has three phonemes /r/, /o/, and /p/. Change one phoneme, say /r/ to /n/, and you have a different word *nope.*

PHONEMIC AWARENESS- the understanding that words are composed of sounds. Phonemic awareness is a specific type of phonological awareness dealing only with phonemes in a spoken word.

PHONICS- the study of relationships between phonemes (speech sounds) and graphemes (letters) that represent the phonemes. It is also decoding or the sounding out of unknown words that are written.

PHONOLOGICAL AWARENESS- the ability to recognize the sounds of spoken language and how they can be blended together, segmented, and switched/manipulated to form new combinations and words.

PHONOLOGICAL CUES- readers use their knowledge of letter/sound and sound/letter relationships to predict and confirm reading.

PHONOLOGY- the study of speech structure in language that includes both the patterns of basic speech units (phonemes) and the tacit rules of pronunciation.

PORTFOLIOS- collections of a child's work over time. They include a cover letter, reflections from the child and teacher, and other supportive documents including standards, performance task examples, prompts, and sometimes peer comments.

PRIMARY LANGUAGE- (ELL term) - the language an individual is the most fluent in and at ease with. This is usually, but not always the individual's first language.

PROMPTS- when the teacher intervenes in the child's independent reading to help the child pronounce or comprehend a specific word or prompt. On a reading record, the teacher notes the prompt. When the teacher wants to match a child with a particular book or determine the child's stage of reading/level, the teacher does not use prompts.

QUESTION GENERATING STRATEGY FOR AN EXPOSITORY TEXT- first the child previews the text by reading titles, subheads, looking at pictures or illustrations, and reading the first paragraph. Next the child asks a "think" question which he or she records. Then the child reads to find information that might answer the "think" question. The child may write down the information found or think about another question that is answered by what the child is reading. The child continues to read using this strategy.

READING FOR INFORMATION- Reading with the purpose of extracting facts and expert opinion from the text. Children should be introduced to the following information reading resources: web resources that are age and grade appropriate for children, the concept of the table of contents, chapter headings, glossaries, pictures, maps, charts, diagrams and text structures in an information text. They should be taught to use notes, graphs, organizers, and mind maps to share information extracted from a text.

RECODE- To change information from one code into another, as recoding writing into oral speech.

RECOGNITION VOCABULARY- the group of words which children are able to correctly pronounce, read orally and understand on sight.

RECORD OF READING BEHAVIOR- (running record) an objective observation during which the teacher records, using a standard set of symbols, everything the child reader says as the child reads a book selected by the teacher.

REFLECTION- to analyze, discuss, and react to one's learning on any grade or age level.

RETELLING- retelling can be written or oral. Children are expected and encouraged to tell as much of a story as they can remember. Re-telling is far more extensive than just summarizing. Children should include the beginning, middle and end plot lines and should be able to tell about the book's characters.

RUBRIC- a set of guidelines or acceptable responses for the completion of any task. Usually a rubric ranges from 0 to 4 with 4 being the most detailed response and 0 indicating a response to the task which lacked detail or was in other ways insufficient.

SCAFFOLDING- refers to the teacher support necessary for the child to accomplish a task or to achieve a goal which the child could not accomplish on his/her own. Vygotsky termed this window of opportunity the "zone of proximal development." Ultimately as the child becomes more proficient or capable, the scaffold is withdrawn. The goal of scaffolding is to help the child to perform the reading task independently and internalize the behavior. During SHARED READING, the task is scaffolded by the teacher's reading to the children aloud. As the teacher reads, the teacher scaffolds the initial decoding and helps with the meaning making/construction.

SEARCHING- children pause to search in the picture, print, or their memory for known information. This can happen as the child tackles an unknown word or after an error.

SECOND LANGUAGE-(ELL term)-A language acquired or learned simultaneously with or after a child's acquisition of a first language.

SEGMENTING- the process of hearing a spoken word and identifying its separate phonemes or syllables.

SELF-CORRECTION- children begin to correct some of their own reading errors. Generally this behavior is accompanied by the re-reading of the previous phrase or sentence.

SEMANTIC CUES- children use their prior knowledge, sense of the story, and pictures to support their predicting and confirming the meaning of the text.

SEMANTIC WEB- a visual graphic organizer that the teacher can use to introduce a reading on a specific topic. It visually represents many other words associated with a target word. The web can help activate the children's prior knowledge and extend or clarify it. It can also serve to check new learning after guided or independent reading.

SPATIAL LEARNING- Using images, color, or layout to help readers whose learning style is spatial.

STANDARD SCORE- how far a child's grade on a standardized test is from the average score (mean) on the test in terms of the standard deviation. If a child scores 70 on a standardized test and the standard deviation is 5 and the average (mean) score is 65, the child is one standard deviation above the average.

STANDARDIZED TEST- a test given under specified conditions allowing comparisons to be made. A set of norms or average scores on this test will be used for comparisons.

STOP AND THINK STRATEGY- a balanced literacy strategy for constructing meaning. As the text is being read, the child asks himself or herself, does this make sense to me? If it does not make sense to me, I should then try to re-read it or read ahead. I can also look up words that I don't know or ask for help. Generally the teacher models this strategy with the whole class as a mini lesson and then it is posted prominently in the classroom for continued reference by the children.

STRATEGIC READERS- as defined by researchers Marie Clay and Sharon Taberski, strategic readers are self improving and do the following as they read:

(A lengthy glossary explanation of this term has been provided because it can appear in a variety of multiple choice questions on the examination as well as part of a constructed response question).

- Monitor their reading to see if it makes sense semantically, syntactically, and visually.
- Look for and use semantic, syntactic, and visual clues.
- Uncover and identify new things about the text.
  Cross check and use one cueing system against another.
- Self-correct their reading when what they first read does not match the semantic, syntactic and visual clues.
- Solve for and identify new words using multiple cueing systems.

Beyond these behaviors, a strategic or self-improving reader uses many strategies to construct meaning. When their reading experience is going well-they know the words and understand the text or story-they are working continuously (even if they are not conscious of it) at maintaining meaning. If and when the strategic or self-improving reader runs into an unfamiliar word, then the reader has many strategies to identify that word. Becoming a successful strategic reader is a goal that can and should be shared with children as early as the middle of the first grade, although the term "self-improving reader" might be used at that point.

TEXT FEATURES- children need to be alerted to the following text features which may initially appear strange to them. The features of text include: a period which marks the end of a "telling sentence;" a question mark that is at the end of a sentence that asks a question, an exclamation mark used to express surprise or excitement at the end of a sentence, capital letters which begin a sentence and the names of persons, places, and things; bold italicized or underlined text to highlight key ideas; quotation marks which show dialogue, a hyphen used to break a long word up into its syllables, a dash used to show a break in an idea, or to indicate a parenthetical element or an omission; an ellipse, which shows an omission or break in the text; and a paragraph in nonfiction which shows a new point being made.

TRANSITIONAL READERS- recognize an increasing number of "hard" words that are content related. They can provide summaries of the stories that they read. They are more at ease with handling longer, more complex, connected text with short chapters. Transitional readers can read independent level texts with correct phrasing, expression, and fluency. When they encounter unfamiliar words, they have a variety of strategies to figure out the unfamiliar words. Their reading demonstrates that they are able to integrate meaning, syntax and phonics in a consistent manner so that they can understand the texts they are reading.

VENN DIAGRAM- a diagram consisting of two or three intersecting circles to visually represent similarities and differences for texts, characters and topics. No author study is complete without VENN DIAGRAMS comparing different author's works. This is the most commonly used graphic organizer in elementary schools today. It can be used effectively as part of an answer to a constructed response question.

VISUAL CUES- readers use their knowledge of graphemes to predict and confirm text. The graphemes may be words, syllables or letters.

WORD ANALYSIS- the analysis of words employing letters, phonic structures, contextual clues, or dictionary skills.

WORD IDENTIFICATION- how the reader determines the pronunciation, and the meaning of an unknown word.

WORD RECOGNITION- The process of determining the pronunciation and some degree of the meaning of an unknown word.

WORD WORK- the term that the balanced literacy approach uses for the study of vocabulary.

"An impressive and growing body of authoritative opinion and research evidence suggests that reading failure is preventable for all but a very small percentage of children."
John Jay Pikulski

Directory of Theorists and Researchers

Introduction:
Many questions on the teacher certification examinations can only be correctly answered if you know the theorist or the research that is referenced. The teaching of reading owes much to the work, principles and guidelines of teacher educators and university field researchers who have changed the style, methods and practice of teaching reading. While those listed in this directory are by no means all the major researchers (page

constraints would make a complete listing impossible), the individuals listed below are those whose contributions are frequently referenced on the certification tests and whose work is evident in today's elementary classroom teaching and learning of reading.

PHONICS CENTERED APPROACH

In 1955 Rudolph Flesch gained national prominence when he published *Why Johnny Can't Read*. This book went on to become a best seller and has now become a classic which is readable and speaks to current concerns. Flesch became the spokesperson for a war that periodically resurfaces in the reading world.

Flesch, Chall (1967) Stahl (1992), Adams (1990), and Johnson and Bauman (1984) believe that a phonics-based approach is crucial for reading success. Flesch and others feel that the balanced literacy advocates are seriously undermining the crucial role that phonics plays in the children's development as successful decoding readers. However, it must be noted that while balanced literacy does emphasize the use of literature based reading programs, it in no way dismisses phonics from its reading program; indeed phonics is included in the crucial "word work" component of the reading and writing workshop.

The phonics advocates point to the fact that most research shows that early and systematic instruction in phonics skills results in superior reading achievement in elementary school and beyond.

Adams (1990) detailed what type of phonics instruction is needed.

To learn to read skillfully, children need practice in seeing and understanding decodable words in real reading situations and with connected text.... phonics instruction {needs to be} part of a reading program that provides ample practice in reading and writing. Encouraging children with connected text can also show them the importance of what they are learning and make the lessons in phonics relevant and sensible. Phonics centered advocates believe that children should begin to learn letter associations in kindergarten with most useful phonics skills being taught by first grade. These basic skills should then be reviewed in second grade and beyond.

Consonant sounds should be taught first, since they are more reliable in their letter-sound associations.

Short vowel sounds appear more frequently in beginning reading materials, so they should be introduced before long vowels. Phonics advocates believe that most beginning readers need to be taught letter sound associations explicitly. Phonics advocates also believe that beginning readers need to read stories that have words to which phonics skills apply. This allows them to practice their phonics skills as they write and spell words. They should also play lots of letter-sound association games.

Phonics advocates claim that when phonics is abandoned reading scores drop and balanced literacy advocates counter with the fact that they have never advocated abandoning the teaching of phonics.

As Jeanne Chall, a professor at Harvard's Graduate School of Education notes: "a beginning reading program that does not give children knowledge and skill in recognizing and decoding words will have poor results."

Theorists and Researchers:

Adams, Marilyn Jaeger

Noted for her research on early reading, Adams lists five basic types of phonemic awareness tasks which should be covered by the end of first grade. These include: ability to hear rhymes and alliterations, ability to do oddity tasks, ability to orally blend words, ability to orally segment words, ability to do phonemic manipulation tasks.

Clay, Marie M. Marie

A New Zealand born researcher, in the field of special needs emergent literacy and in the development of assessment tools for these children. Her research in this field is felt throughout the Reading Recovery movement and involves the use of her, *Reading Recovery: A Guidebook for Teachers in Training,* in the majority of graduate emergent literacy courses and in many classrooms in the US including those that do not have a Reading Recovery teacher.

Her doctoral thesis focused on what was to become her life's work, emergent reading behavior. At the crux of her research for the dissertation, Clay reviewed and detailed the progress week by week of one hundred children during their first year of school (1966). An important outcome of the dissertation was her development of reliable observation tools for the assessment and analysis of changes over time in children's literacy learning. These assessments are the crux of *An Observation Survey of Early Literacy Achievement* (1993) which is an essential work for the primary school educator. The assessments have been validated and reconstructed for learners from the Spanish, Maori and French languages. A special appendix in this guide includes the *Record of Reading Behavior* tool she created with Kenneth Goodman.

Reading Recovery is a key Clay contribution to the field of foundations of reading teaching. The movement, which is discussed in detail in this section, was born out of the concerns of classroom educators who were upset that even with excellent programs and expert teaching, they were not able to positively influence the literacy progress of some of their young children. Clay posed the question of investigating what would happen if the design and delivery of traditional reading education were changed for these struggling young learners.

The whole thrust of the Reading Recovery movement has been to improve the early identification and instructional delivery for these struggling young readers. Her goal was to develop a system which would bring those children scoring the lowest in assessment measures to the level of the average readers within their classes.

With the support of Barbara Watson and others, the program was developed in three years. The first field tests of the program took place in the late 1970's in Auckland schools. To date, circa 2005, the program is operating in most English speaking countries and has been reconstructed for use in Spanish and French.

Janet S. Gaffey and Billie Askew have said of Marie Clay (1991) that her contribution "has been to change what is possible for individual learners when teaching permits different routes to be taken for desired outcomes."

Reading Recovery has been identified by the International Reading Association as a program that not only teaches children how to read, but also reduces the number of children who are labeled as "learning disabled." It further lowers the number of children who are placed in remedial reading programs and classes.

Clay Reading Recovery lessons are designed to promote accelerated learning so that children can catch up to their peers and continue to learn independently.

The hallmark of the Reading Recovery program is that the Reading Recovery teacher works with one student at a time over a 12 to 20 week period. Each daily 30 minute lesson is tailored to address the needs of the individual student. Therefore Reading Recovery teachers generally teach no more than four or five students per day in individual lessons.

The Clay Observation of Early Childhood Achievement (1993) is used to assess children's strengths and weaknesses. Reading Recovery teachers devote the first ten minutes of their sessions with individual children to assessment as the children engage in reading and writing. A running record of the child's progress is taken every day and is used to plan future lessons.

The lessons themselves include the use of familiar stories. Children engage in assembling and in sequencing cut up stories. They work with letters or write a story. Teaching style involves the teacher demonstrating strategies and the child then developing effective strategies to continue reading independently. Key components of each lesson include: phonemic awareness, phonics, spelling, and comprehension study. Much time is devoted to problem solving so that the children's decoding is purposeful. Children are given time to practice and demonstrate fluency skills.

Ultimately what sets Reading Recovery aside is the fact that it is one-to-one tutoring. This is also what makes it effective for children, and of course, what raises issues about it are costs for the school systems which may want to adopt it. Obviously the districts and education systems have to decide whether they want to pay the costs of this and other individualized tutoring systems now in the primary school years or pay later as these children become adults whose literacy skills are not sufficient for proactive citizenship.

Fountas, Irene C and Gay Su Pinnell
These two researchers have developed a leveling system for reading texts, which arranges them by level of difficulty. Beyond a specific analysis of set titles, the theorists have explained in several published works how to use their leveling system to meet and assess

the progress of various readers. They also provide detailed explanations and support for reading teachers of young children K-3 in using reading records and benchmark texts.

They are the key articulators of the balanced literacy model that includes reading and writing workshop. Among their other contributions to the field are: guidelines for creating sets of leveled books, assessment rubrics, strategies for fostering "word solver" skills in child readers, and methods for teaching phonics and spelling in the literacy classroom.

Routman, Regie

Routman's contributions to Reading Foundations are the result of over three decades of experience as an elementary school teacher, a reading specialist, a learning disabilities tutor, a Reading Recovery teacher, a language arts and mentor teacher and a staff developer. Due to these various experiences, her insights into reading resonate with a broad spectrum of school community members.

Routman's works are conversational, teacher-to-teacher sharings of her daily experiences in classrooms. In her published books on the teaching of reading (i.e. *Reading Essentials*-Heinemann, 2002), Regie shows teachers how to teach consistent with the findings in reading research, yet also with highly practical "scripted lessons" and teaching tips which make the classroom come alive. She advocates literature based teaching and meaning centered approaches for learning.

In addition, she is a strong advocate of using poetry from grades one and beyond as an integral thread for a reading program. She is the author of *Kids' Poems: Teaching Children to Love Writing Poetry* (Scholastic, 2000) which includes separate volumes of poetry for grades K-4.

Routman believes in teaching reading to meet specific children's needs regardless of the particular reading program in place. She is a strong advocate for the use of small guided reading groups and reading for understanding. Phonics and other word analysis strategies are part of her reading framework, but not at its core. Her focus for the reading classroom is on the development and the use of the classroom library as the center for an independent reading program, shared reading and reading aloud.

Routman has designed informal reading evaluations on books/texts her students are reading (her published works are known for their appendices replete with templates for evaluations, projects, reports, book lists, suggested texts by topics etc.). Her classroom model includes matching children with specific library books as well as linking assessment with instruction. Finally she is a researcher who sees reading as intimately linked to writing. Routman is also involved with the politics of literacy. This vision of literacy involves the image of the teacher, as an informed professional, who regularly reads the latest professional books, collaborates with colleagues in school and beyond, and deals with the most recent research developments. Interestingly, Routman is one researcher who also feels that an informed professional can and should know when to question research. Other aspects of the politics of literacy as Routman conceptualizes them are: communicating effectively with parents and dealing with testing and standards mandates.

Two of her published works, *Conversations: Strategies for Teaching, Learning, and Evaluating* (Heinemann, 2000) and *Invitations: Changing as Teachers and Learners k-12* (Heinemann, 1991 and 1994) are essential for the elementary reading teacher's bookshelf and can take the teacher through several years of work.

Taberski, Sharon

Taberski is an experienced elementary teacher educator who is also a member of the Primary Literacy Standards Committee run by the National Center on Education and the Economy and the University of Pittsburgh. Her works in the field are served up as wonderfully accessible and necessary advice from "the veteran teacher across the hall" who loves her students and is delighted to help a new colleague.

Unlike many theorists in the field of reading, Taberski's work is not focused around a prescribed set of skills, but rather around a series of interconnected interactions with the learner.

Among these interactions which are detailed and clearly communicated in her book *On Solid Ground* (2000-Heinemann) are:

- Assessment- Procedures for assessing children's reading, and to inform teaching, scheduling and managing reading conferences, taking oral reading records, and using retellings as discussion tools.
- Demonstration- Taberski developed and field tested strategies for using shared reading and read aloud as platforms for figuring out words and comprehending texts. She is a strong advocate of small group work-guided reading, word-study groups and teaching children one on one.
- Practice- In the Taberski framework, independent reading is used as a time for practice. Students play key roles in this practice and Sharon has a set of detailed and easily adaptable guidelines for matching children with books for independent reading. Her work includes booklists and ready to use information that is available for reproduction.
- Response- It's important for students to know that they are doing well and where they must focus their efforts to improve skills. Taberski explains how her students use writing and dialogue as tools for independent reading.

Vail, Priscilla

Noted for her research in the study of dyslexia and its myths, Vail has articulated ways in which children can develop their reading skills as they cope with this disorder and techniques parents and educators can use to support reading development. She has also worked on specific test taking skills for children coping with dyslexia and other special needs. Her strategies can be infused in the regular education program to enhance all students' reading achievement schools. She is a proponent of phonics instruction and skills within the context of an integrated whole language approach (once called integrated language arts).

Another focus of Vail's research is the link between language and thinking. She is concerned with how a child's receptive language, expressive language and metacognition can be fostered. She has developed assessment methods for each of these capacities and activities to help strengthen them in children grades K-4.

BIBLIOGRAPHY OF PRINT RESOURCES

PROFESSIONAL BOOKS:

Adams, M. (1990). *Beginning to read: Thinking and Learning about Print.* Cambridge, MA: MIT Press.

Anders, P., & Bos, C. (1986). Semantic Feature Analysis: An Interactive Strategy for Vocabulary Development and Reading Comprehension, *Journal of Reading*, 29, 610-616.

Blevins, W. (1997). *Phonemic Awareness Activities for Early Reading Success.* New York: Scholastic.

Boyd-Bastone, P. (2004). Focused Anecdotal Record Assessment (ARA): A Tool for Standards Based Authentic Assessment. *Reading Teacher, 58* (3), pp. 230-239.

Calkins, Lucy McCormick. (2001). *The Art of Teaching Reading.* New York: Longman. This is the woman who beautifully explains the reading workshop and its relationship to the writing workshop as she shares wonderful snapshots of mini lessons, conferring, conferencing, independent reading, guided reading, book talks, prompts, coaching, and classroom library use. Exceedingly readable and direct.

Campbell, Robin. (2004). *Reading and Writing for Real Purposes.* Portsmouth, NH: Heinemann.
This work focuses on how children who deftly absorb and interconnect symbols and sounds of their universes can be supported in K-1 classes to extend this ability into phonics learning. Campbell demonstrates how immersion in a highly literate classroom filled with print and language stimuli allows kids to build accurate letter-sound relationships. The book provides a framework for teaching phonics using proven field-tested Campbell strategies.

Among these strategies are: early mark making, read-alouds, playing with language in rhyme and song, writing and reading in a variety of genres, exploring environmental and classroom print, and using students' own names. Samples of student work are included.

Chancey, C. (1994). Language development, metalinguistic awareness, and emergent literacy skills of 3 year old children in relation to social class. *Applied Psycholinguistics*, 15, 371-394.

Clay, Marie M. (1993). *An Observation Survey of Early Literacy Achievement.* Portsmouth, NH: Heinemann.

Clay, Marie M. (1993). *Reading Recovery: A Guidebook for Teachers in Training.* Portsmouth, NH: Heinemann.

Cooper, J. David. (2004). *Literacy-Helping Children Construct Meaning.* Boston, MA: Houghton Mifflin. (5th Edition).

> This book explains with numerous charts, tables, templates, and excerpts form actual texts, what the balanced literacy approach to the teaching of reading and writing is. It offers the new teacher: exact schedules, strategies, guidelines, assessment tools, bibliographies, research, and even scripts for conferring with children.
>
> Cooper is a clear and crisp writer who does not overwhelm the reader, but rather engages the reader. Even veteran teachers would return again and again to this text for support and refreshing insights.

Cox, Carole. (2005). *Teaching Language Arts.* Boston, MA: Pearson.

> A compendium of state of the art lesson plans, web resources, online case studies, teaching ideas and extensive templates. All of these materials are aligned to the balanced literacy reading and writing workshop model.
>
> The book also includes teaching ideas for the ELL reader, children with learning disabilities, and speakers of non- standard dialects. The book also features snapshots of second language learners as well as bi-literacy web resources.

Cullinan, Bernice E. (1998). *Three Voices-An Invitation to Poetry Across the Curriculum.* New York: Stenhouse. K-6 and beyond.

> Two classroom educators and a noted researcher in children's literature demonstrate how poetry can be used in the classroom to teach various aspects of reading and to nurture lifelong literacy. Thirty-three grade and age appropriate strategies are included which have been field tested in classrooms across the country.

Ezell, H. K., & Justice, L. M. (2000). Increasing the Print Focus of Adult -Child Shared Book Reading through Observational Learning. *American journal of Speech Pathology,* 9, 36-37.

Flesch, Rudolf. (1985). *Why Johnny Can't Read.* New York: Harper and Row.

Fountas, Irene C., & Gay Su Pinnell. (2001). *Guiding Readers and Writers 3-6.* Portsmouth, NH: Heinemann.

> This work includes 1000 leveled books with guidelines for using them as part of a reading and writing workshop. The book explains how to use various genres in the classroom and how to use visual graphic organizers for the teaching of reading and writing.

Fountas, Irene. C., & Gay Su Pinnell. (1999). *Matching Books to Readers Using Leveled Books in Guided Reading K-3.* Portsmouth, NH: Heinemann.

> This major contribution to the field has a list of 7, 500 grade and age appropriate books. In addition the authors include word counts to be used for keeping running records, text characteristics, guidelines for leveling of additional books and suggestions for developing classroom library collections.

> Other works by these researchers also published by Heinemann include:
> *Voices on Word matters: Learning about Phonics and Spelling in the Literacy Classroom* (1999) and *Word Matters-Teaching Phonics and Spelling in the Reading/Writing Classroom* (1998).

Fry, Edward Bernard, Jacqueline Kress, Dona Lee Fountakidis, (2000). *The Reading Teacher's Book of Lists.* San Francisco, CA: Wiley Press.

> This book is an invaluable one for the working classroom educator. It includes ready to use lists that cover a multiplicity of teacher needs. Among them are: spelling demons, readability graphs, phonics, useful words, reading math, vowel lists, anagrams, portmanteaus (do you know what they are and how well they can work in word study?), web sites, classic children's literature, etc. Even a veteran teacher educator will find useful and new resources. Also wonderful for developing independent word study investigations and literature explorations.

Ganske, Kathy. (2000). *Word Journeys-Assessment-Guided Phonics, Spelling, and Vocabulary Instruction.* New York, NY: Guilford Press.

> This book offers a practical approach for assessing children's spelling. The author has created a DSA (Development Spelling Analysis) tool which teachers can use to evaluate individual children's spelling progress and to differentiate instruction. The book includes snapshots of children at different levels of spelling development.

Hall, Susan. (1994). *Using Picture Books to Teach Literary Devices.* Westport, CT: Oryx Press.

How to Help Every Child Become a Reader. Just Publishing. K-6 and beyond.

> This accessible text draws on materials developed by the US Department of Education to share research, resources, referrals and suggestions for supporting all children to become lifelong and engaged readers. It offers specific suggestions and resources for assisting struggling readers including those with special needs and those from ELL backgrounds.

Labov, L. (2003). When Ordinary Children Fail to Read. *Reading Research Quarterly,* 38, 128-31.

Macmillan, B. M. (2002). Rhyme and Reading. A Critical Review of the Research Methodology. *Journal of Research in Reading,* 25(1), 4-42.

Makor, Barbara. *Primary Phonics Readers.*

Short storybooks that K-2 can own and read independently.

They feature phonetically controlled texts, sounds and spellings that are grade and age appropriate and high interest child-centered themes. As children progress through the series of twenty titles, they review and enhance their mastery of phonetic elements, sight words, and sequences at a more rapid pace. This material is compatible with the majority of phonics programs.

Munro, J. (1998). Phonological and Phonemic Awareness: Their Impact on Learning to Read Prose and Spell. *Australian Journal of Learning Disabilities*, 3, 2, 15-21.

Paperback Nursery Rhyme Sampler-Whispering Coyote Press-
Essential for a Prek-1 classroom and useful even in grades 1 and 2; these classic nursery rhymes promote phonemic and phonological awareness and children's ownership of their reading through song and movement.

Routman, Regie. (2000). *Conversations: Strategies for Teaching, Learning, and Evaluating.* Portsmouth, NH: Heinemann.

Routman, Regie. (1994). *Invitations: Changing as Teachers and Learners K-12.* Portsmouth, NH. Heinemann.

Routman, Regie. (1996). *Literacy at the Crossroads: Crucial Talk about Reading, Writing, and Other Teaching Dilemmas.* Portsmouth, NH: Heinemann.

Routman, Regie. (2002). *Reading Essentials*. Portsmouth, NH: Heinemann.

Statman, Ann. *Handprints-Leveled Storybooks for Early Readers Educators Publishing Service*-Grades K-2.

These fifty titles which come with five teacher's guides were leveled using the Fountas and Pinnell Guided Reading Leveling System. The stories reflect real world situations and people young readers know. They include: sentence structure, pictures and cues that focus strategic reading. Print size, sentence positioning, and word spacing is appropriate for the level of the particular storybook. The titles build a strong sight vocabulary through the use of high frequency words. Language used within the series progresses from natural to formal book language.

Schumm, Heanne Shay. *The Reading Tutor's Handbook*. Free Spirit. K-6 and beyond.

This guide offers step by step instructions, templates and handouts for providing children with differentiated reading support. It is not only helpful for teachers, but also can be shared with paraprofessionals, teachers, interns, and parents as a support framework for the classroom reading program.

Taberski, Sharon. (2000). *On Solid Ground: Creating a Literacy Environment in Your K-3 Classroom.* Portsmouth, NH: Heinemann.

Terban, Marvin. *Time to Rhyme-A Rhyming Dictionary*. Boyd Mills Press. Grades 1-3.

This book is easily enough formatted so that it can be used to introduce children in the early elementary grades to the use of a rhyming dictionary as a reference tool. Its simple word groupings encourage writing which can also reinforce and reciprocally enhance reading skills through the reading and writing workshop.

Vail, Patricia. *Reading Comprehension-Students Needs and Teacher's Tools.* Educators Publishers Service K-6 and beyond.

This is a compendium of explanations of specific instructional practices, terms, student projects, learning games and resources which are critical for successfully teaching reading

TOOLS TO HELP YOU TEACH THE FOUNDATIONS OF READING AND SUCCEEDING IN CONSTRUCTED RESPONSE CERTIFICATION EXAMINATIONS

Appendix 1- The Record of Reading Behavior- A close up look at a key assessment tool.

Often in the constructed response question on a foundations of education certification test or on a general elementary certification test, the educator is asked to analyze a record of reading behavior or to construct an appropriate one from data given in an anecdote. Furthermore with the current climate of accountability, it is a good idea for new teachers and for career changers to examine closely the basic elements of recording reading behavior.

While there are various acceptable formats for emergent literacy assessment used throughout the country, the one selected for use here is based on the work of Marie Clay and Kenneth Goodman. These two are key researchers in the close observation and documentations of children's early reading miscues (reading mistakes).

It is important to emphasize that the teacher should not just "take the Record of Reading Behavior "and begin filling it out as the child reads from a random book prior to beginning of the observation. There are specific steps for taking the record and analyzing its results.

1. Select a text
If you want to see if the child is reading on instructional level, choose a book that the child has already read. If the purpose of the test is to see whether the child is ready to advance to the next level, choose a book from that level which the child has not yet seen.

2. Introduce the text
If the book is one that has been read, you do not need to introduce the text, other than by saying the title. But if the book is new to the child, you should briefly share the title and tell the child a bit about the plot and style of the book.

3. Take the record

Generally with emergent readers' grades 1-2, there are only 100-150 words in a passage used to take a record. Make certain that the child is seated beside you, so that you can see the text as the child reads it.

If desired, you may want to photocopy the text in advance for yourself, so you can make direct notations on your text while the child reads from the book.

After you introduce the text make certain that the child has the chance to read the text independently. Be certain that you do not "teach" or help the child with the text, other than to supply an unknown word that the child requests you supply. The purpose of the record is to see what the child does on his or her own.

As the child reads the text, you must be certain to record the reading behaviors the child exhibits using the following notations.

In taking the record, keep in mind the following: Allow enough time for the child to work independently on a problem before telling or supplying the word. If you wait too long, you could run the risk of having the child lose the meaning and his/her interest in the story as he or she tries to identify the unknown word.

It is recommended that when a child is way off track, you tell him or her to "Try that again" (TTA). If a whole phrase is troubling, put it into square brackets and score it as only one error.

The notation for filling out the Record of Reading behavior involves noting the child's response on the top with the actual text below it.

Comprehension Check

This can and should be done by inviting the child to retell the story. This retelling can then be used to ask further questions about characters, plot, setting and purpose which allow you to observe and to record the child's level of comprehension.

Calculating the Reading Level and the Self-correction Rate

Calculating the reading level lets you know if the book is at the level on which the child can read it independently or comfortably with guidance or if the book is at a level where reading it frustrates the child.

Generally, an accuracy score of 95-100% suggests that the child can read the text and other books or texts on the same level.

An accuracy score of 90-94% indicates that the text and texts likely will present challenges to the child, but with guidance from you, a tutor or parent, the child will be able to master these texts and enjoy them. This is instructional level.

However, an accuracy score of less than 89% tells you that the material you have selected for the child is too hard for the child to control alone. Such material needs to be shared with the child in a shared reading situation or read to the child.

KEEPING SCORE ON THE RECORD

Insertions, omissions, substitutions, and teacher told responses, all count as errors. Repetitions are not scored as errors. Corrected responses are scored as self corrections.

No penalty is given for a child's attempts at self correction that results in a finally incorrect response but the attempts should be noted. Multiple unsuccessful attempts at a word score as one error only.

The lowest score for any page is zero.

If a child omits a line or lines, each word omitted is counted as an error. If the child omits a page, deduct the number of words omitted from the total number of words which you have used for the record.

Calculating the Reading Level

Note the number of errors made on each line on the Record of Reading Behavior in the column marked E (for Error).

Total the number of errors in the text and divide this number into the number of words that the child has read. This will give you the error rate.

If a child read a passage of 100 words and made 10 errors, the error rate would be 1 in 10. Convert this to an accuracy percentage, or 90%.

Calculating the Self Correction Rate

Total all the self-corrections.

Next, add the number of errors to the number of self-corrections and divide by the number of self-corrections.

A self correction rate of 1 in 3 to 1 in 5 is considered good. This rate indicates that the child is able to help him- or herself as problems are encountered in reading.

Analyzing the record

This record should assist the educator in developing a detailed date specific picture of the child's progress in reading behavior. It should be used to help the educator individualize instruction for the specific child.

As the errors are reviewed, consider whether the child made the error because of semantics (cues from meaning), syntactic (language structure), or visual information difficulties.

As self-corrections are analyzed, consider what led the child to make that self-correction. Check out and consider what cues the child does use effectively and which the child does not use well.

Consider the ways in which the child tackles a word which is unknown. Characterize that behavior and consider how the teacher can assist the child with this issue.

If a child can retell at least three quarters of a story, this is considered adequate for retelling.

Analysis of reading behavior records can and should support the educator in designing appropriate mini lessons and strategies to help the child with his or her recorded errors and miscues.

Sample Test

1. The major difference between phonemic and phonological awareness is: *(Easy) (Skill 1.1)*

   A) One deals with a series of discrete sounds and the other with sound-spelling relationships.

   B) One is involved with teaching and learning alliteration and rhymes.

   C) Phonemic awareness is a specific type of phonological awareness that deals with separate phonemes within a given word.

   D) Phonological awareness is associated with printed words.

2. Mr. Sanchez is having his students work with one-syllable words, removing the first consonant and substituting another, as in m/ats to h/ats. What reading skill are they working on? *(Average rigor) (Skill 1.1)*

   A) Morphemic inflections.

   B) Pronouncing short vowels.

   C) Invented spelling.

   D) Phonological awareness.

3. Most of the children in first-year teacher Ms. James's class are really doing well in their phonemic awareness assessments. However, Ms. James is very concerned about three children who do not seem to be able to distinguish between spoken words that "sound alike," but are different. Since she is a first year teacher, she feels her inexperience may be to blame. In truth, the reason these three children have not yet demonstrated phonemic awareness is most likely that: *(Rigorous) (Skill 1.1)*

   A) They are not capable of becoming good readers.

   B) They may have problems paying attention.

   C) They may be from an ELL background.

   D) Ms. James does not pronounce the different phonemes clearly enough.

4. Gracie seems to be struggling with her reading, even in first grade, although her mother works at a publishing firm and her dad is an editor. Her speech is also full of mispronunciations, although her parents were born in the school neighborhood. Gracie should be checked by: *(Average rigor) (Skill 1.1)*

    A) A reading specialist.

    B) A speech therapist or an audiologist

    C) A pediatrician.

    D) A psychologist.

5. Ronald's parents are hearing-impaired. What work will this first grader need most? *(Rigorous) (Skill 1.1)*

    A) Picture cues to promote visual acuity.

    B) Sight word mastery to promote fluency.

    C) Rhymes and read alouds to promote phonological awareness.

    D) Letter-sound practice to promote the alphabetic principle.

6. The most important reason to keep ongoing assessments of children's phonological awareness is: *(Rigorous) (Skill 1.1)*

    A) To be accountable to the principal.

    B) To compare with teachers of the same grade level.

    C) To have data for report cards.

    D) To plan curriculum.

7. A stationery store owner in the neighborhood of the school is amused by the fact that the children on a school walk, are rushing up to various store signs and street signs. The children are probably exploring: *(Average rigor) (Skill 1.1)*

    A) The alphabetic principle.

    B) The principle that print carries meaning.

    C) Letter sound recognition.

    D) Phonemic awareness.

8. Clapping is the best way to learn syllable divisions because: *(Rigorous) (Skill 1.1)*

    A) Children enjoy the activity and are motivated to learn.

    B) Syllables are rhythmic.

    C) The activity is both auditory and kinesthetic.

    D) Movement aids memory.

9. Arrange these phenomena in the order in which they are mastered by children in reading: (Rigorous) (Skill 1.2)

A) Environmental print, alphabetic principle, phonological awareness, decoding.

B) Environmental print, phonological awareness, alphabetic principle, decoding.

C) Environmental print, decoding, alphabetic principle, phonological awareness.

D) Environmental print, phonological awareness, decoding, alphabetic principle.

10. The value of allowing children to use invented spelling? (Rigorous) (Skill 1.2)

A) It frees up the teacher to get around to many children during Writing Workshop.

B) It ultimately contributes to good spelling skills.

C) It helps children listen to the sounds of words they are attempting to write.

D) It makes children feel proud of their writing.

11. It is 4 PM, yet Francine is still in her classroom. The seats in her classroom are filled with adults of various ages who are holding books. They are seated two by two with both holding copies of the same book. Francine probably is: (Average rigor) (Skill 1.2)

A) Explaining to parents how she will teach a particular story.

B) Demonstrating shared reading with a buddy for volunteer parents.

C) Hosting a parents' organization meeting for her grade level.

D) Distributing old books from the class library to parents.

12. Chard and Osborn (1999) found that children with reading disabilities need to learn the alphabetic principle because: (Rigorous) (Skill 1.2)

A) The alphabet has predictable letter-sound relationships.

B) Learning sight words is harder for the disabled reader.

C) Knowing the alphabet will give these readers confidence.

D) The relationship between letters and sounds is central to early reading.

13. _____ is to letter-sound relationships as _____ is to word meanings. (Rigorous) *(Skill 1.2)*

   A) Decoding; syntax.

   B) Phonological awareness; phonemic awareness.

   C) Syntax; semantics.

   D) Graphophonemic awareness; semantics.

14. **The purpose of taking dictation is to:** (Easy) *(Skill 1.2)*

   A) Demonstrate how to copy down speech.

   B) Make a connection and promote awareness of the relationship between spoken and written language.

   C) Authenticate the children's comments.

   D) Raise the children's self-esteem.

15. **To encode means that you:** (Easy) *(Skill 1.2)*

   A) Decode a second time.

   B) Construct meaning from a code.

   C) Tell someone a message.

   D) None of the above.

16. **Once a teacher has carefully recorded and documented a running record:** (Average rigor) *(Skill 1.2)*

   A) There is nothing further to do as long as the teacher keeps the running record for conferences and documentation of grades.

   B) The teacher should review the running record and other subsequent ones taken for growth over time.

   C) The teacher should differentiate instruction for that particular student as indicated by growth over time and evidence of other needs.

   D) Both B and C.

17. **Rudolf Flesch is to _____ as Marie Clay is to _____.** (Rigorous) *(Skill 1.3)*

   A) Cultural literacy; balanced literacy.

   B) Decodable books; leveled books.

   C) Phonics; Reading Recovery.

   D) Wordless picture books; picture story books.

18. Cues in reading are: (Average rigor) *(Skill 1.3)*

A) Vowel sounds.

B) Digraphs.

C) Sources of information used by readers to help them construct meaning.

D) Tips given by the teacher.

19. Asking a child if what he or she has read makes sense to him or her prompts the child to use: (Average rigor) *(Skill 1.3)*

A) Phonics cues.

B) Syntactic cues.

C) Semantic cues.

D) Prior knowledge.

20. When they are in 6ᵗʰ grade, children should be able to independently go through an unfamiliar collection and: (Average rigor) *(Skill 1.3)*

A) Use only the table of contents.

B) Use the first line indices, and find a poem by author and subject.

C) Use only the glossary.

D) Read bar graphs but not pie charts.

21. One of the most important features in nonfiction books that children should learn to read includes: (Rigorous) *(Skill 1.3)*

A) Page numbers.

B) Picture cues.

C) Characterization.

D) Captions.

22. As the visitors from the United Kingdom tour the school, they are pleased to hear a sing-song chant "Don't fall asleep at the page, don't forget the _____" Mr. Adams explains to them that the first graders are learning about pointing at words and moving from the left to the right. This is called: (Easy) *(Skill 1.3)*

A) Directionality.

B) Return sweep.

C) Top to bottom.

D) Line for line reading.

23. Environmental print is available in all of the following except: (Rigorous) *(Skill 1.3)*

A) Within a newspaper.

B) On the page of a library book.

C) On a supermarket circular.

D) In a commercial flyer.

24. **Children learn book- handling skills best through: (Rigorous) (Skill 1.3)**

    A) Teacher modeling during shared reading.

    B) Parents reading to their children at home.

    C) Imitation of book buddies or peer tutors from another class.

    D) Direct instruction by the teacher.

25. **The best way for a primary grade teacher to model directionality and one to one word matching would be: (Average rigor) (Skill 1.3)**

    A) Using a regular library or classroom text book.

    B) Using her own personal reading book.

    C) Using a big book.

    D) Using a book dummy.

26. **To decode is to: (Easy) (Skill 1.3)**

    A) Construct meaning

    B) Sound out a printed sequence of letters.

    C) Use a special code to decipher a message.

    D) Write out what one hears.

27. **By definition, which children in a classroom will have trouble with syntactic cues? (Rigorous) (Skill 1.3)**

    A) Those from families who do not have household libraries.

    B) Those not in a top reading group.

    C) Those from ELL backgrounds.

    D) All of the above.

28. **A natural role for a highly proficient reader would be: (Average rigor) (Skill 1.3)**

    A) To assist the teacher with cleaning the classroom and organizing the student folders.

    B) To develop charts for the teacher by copying needed poems for full class study.

    C) Tutor and support struggling readers.

    D) Work on his/her own interests while the teacher works with the rest of the class.

29. Based on individual conferences with many children, the teacher realizes that although they are all self-improving readers, they need help in better use of the context to define words. The teacher decided to try the use of: (Average rigor) *(Skill 1.3)*

A) A dictionary to look up words.

B) A thesaurus to use with the dictionary.

C) Contextual redefinition training.

D) Instruction in how to effectively use a dictionary.

30. To promote word study, children can: (Average rigor) *(Skill 1.4)*

A) Be required to go to the dictionary at least once or twice a day.

B) Collect and share words of interest they find in their readings.

C) Do vocabulary work sheets from a basal reader or commercial vocabulary book.

D) Do all of the above.

31. In order to get children to compile specialized vocabulary, they can use: (Average rigor) *(Skill 1.4)*

A) Newspapers.

B) Internet resources and approved web-sites that focus on their special interest.

C) Experts they can interview.

D) All of the above.

32. Teachers should select at least ___ ___words for pre-reading vocabulary discussion: (Easy) *(Skill 1.4)*

A) 12.

B) 15.

C) 2-3.

D) 8-10.

33. The word "bat" is a ___word for "batter-up": (Rigorous) *(Skill 1.4)*

A) Suffix.

B) Prefix.

C) Root word.

D) Inflectional ending.

34. An effective way to build vocabulary and to make connections with mandated science and mathematics material is to teach Greek and Latin roots using: (Average rigor) *(Skill 1.4)*

    A) Semantic maps.

    B) Hierarchical arrays.

    C) Linear arrays.

    D) Word webs.

35. To help children with "main idea" questions, the teacher should: (Average rigor) *(Skill 1.4)*

    A) Give out a strategy sheet on the main idea for children to place their reader's notebooks.

    B) Model responding to such a question as part of guided reading.

    C) Have children create "main idea questions" to go with their writings

    D) All of the above.

36. Dictionary study: (Average rigor) *(Skill 1.4)*

    A) Can begin in grades 1 or 2.

    B) Can begin in pre-K using the lush picture dictionaries.

    C) Should start on grade three level.

    D) A and B.

37. An excellent research project that can combine dictionary study with science research would be: (Average rigor) *(Skill 1.4)*

    A) A student-authored dictionary with terms and phrases about earthworms.

    B) A teacher developed specialized dictionary of words and phrases about earthworms.

    C) A collection of articles on earthworms put together by the school librarian.

    D) B and C.

38. Mr. Adams has complained to Mr. Mark that there are too many newspapers piled up in his classroom. Mr. Mark has responded that he does not want to throw away these piled up newspapers because: (Average rigor) *(Skill 1.4)*

    A) They can be used for letter – sound correspondence.

    B) They represent environmental print.

    C) They can be used to create print-meaning signs.

    D) All of the above.

39. Sometimes children can be asked to demonstrate their understanding of a text in a non-written format. This might include all of the following except: (Rigorous) *(Skill 2.5)*

A) A story map.

B) A Venn diagram.

C) Storyboarding a part of the story with dialogue bubbles.

D) Retelling or paraphrasing.

40. The concerned parent whose child had a visual impairment wanted as much help for him as the teacher and the school district could give her. She begged: "Please, he didn't attend pre-school, he has no prior knowledge. Strictly speaking this is: (Average rigor) *(Skill 2.5)*

A) Correct, since he didn't get pre-school experiences.

B) Incorrect, since prior knowledge covers everyone's experiences.

C) Incorrect, since he did have prior knowledge experiences but these didn't match those of many of his peers, so he would need to enhance his prior knowledge.

D) B and C.

41. Randy is proud of how many new vocabulary words he has learned. He enjoys playing with a device his teacher has, since it helps him to show all the words he can create from various letters. The device is a: (Average rigor) *(Skill 2.5)*

A) Word strip.

B) Letter holder for making words.

C) Word mask.

D) Computer.

42. "Beautiful Beth is the Best Girl in the Bradley Bay area." This sentence could be used to help children learn about: (Average rigor) *(Skill 2.5)*

A) Assonance.

B) Alliteration.

C) Rhyming pairs.

D) None of the above.

43. A district observer notes that fifth graders are showing younger peers in the third grade how to hold a book and walk around with it, they assume: (Average rigor) *(Skill 2.5)*

A) That the fifth graders are particularly theatrical.

B) That the fifth graders are proud of how they read stories aloud.

C) That the fifth graders are training the younger children in book holding.

D) That this has nothing to do with instruction.

44. When you ask a child if what he or she has just read "sounds right" to him or her, you are trying to get that child to use: (Average rigor) *(Skill 2.5)*

A) Phonics cues.

B) Syntactic cues.

C) Semantic cues.

D) Prior knowledge.

45. Children "own" words when all of the following happen except: (Easy) *(Skill 2.5)*

A) They find these words on their own.

B) The teacher provides a mandated word list.

C) They use the words in their own writings.

D) The words appear in literature that interests them.

46. Pre-teaching vocabulary is to___ ___as choral reading is to (Rigorous) (Skill 2.5)

A) Comprehension; letter-sound relationships.

B) Fluency; articulation.

C) Esthetic appreciation; comprehension.

D) Comprehension; fluency.

47. Before selecting words for study, a teacher might: (Easy) *(Skill 2.5)*

A) Read the story and complete story mapping.

B) Ask advice from a veteran teacher and the grade leader.

C) Look in a teacher's guide and choose important concepts listed there.

D) All of the above are correct

48. A teacher discovers after considering his class's prior knowledge of the story material that he would need to teach 12 words at least before he starts teaching the story to the whole group. This indicates: (Average rigor) *(Skill 2.5)*

A) The children will need a read-aloud.

B) The children will need independent reading.

C) The children will need guided reading.

D) The children will need shared reading.

49. The teacher is working on a life science unit in grade five and using many print and electronic sources for information. Some of the words in the unit have a serial and others a categorical relationship to one another. To help the children's comprehension, the teacher could now: (Rigorous) *(Skill 2.5)*

A) Use a root family diagram or tree.

B) Work with base words.

C) Use hierarchical and linear arrays.

D) Create separate semantic maps of each word.

50. Direct teaching of a concept or strategy means: (Average rigor) *(Skill 2.5)*

A) The teacher teaches the concept or strategy as part of a genre lesson.

B) The teacher teaches the concept as part of the writing workshop.

C) The teacher explicitly announces to the class that this strategy will be taught.

D) The teacher teaches the strategy to a small group of children or to an individual child.

51. The substitute teacher starts reading aloud the Big Book (which she has never seen before) on the easel. What do you predict will happen? (Rigorous) *(Skill 2.5)*

A) The children will enjoy hearing the book read by another voice.

B) The teacher's unfamiliarity will lead her to ask excellent prediction questions.

C) The teacher will be excited by what she spontaneously discovers in the book.

D) The teacher will not read very expressively nor will she have a clear purpose for reading the book.

52. As Ms. Wolmark looks at the mandated vocabulary curriculum for the 6th grade, she notes that she can opt to teach foreign words and abbreviations which have become part of the English language. She decides: (Rigorous) *(Skill 2.5)*

A) To forego that since she is not a teacher of foreign language.

B) To teach only foreign words from the native language of her four ELL students.

C) To use the ELL students' native languages as a start for an extensive study of foreign language words.

D) To teach a minimal number of foreign language words that are now in English.

53. As Mr. Adams exits the school building, he notices that Mr. Mark, a new teacher, is leading a group of happy-looking fifth graders back into the building. They are carrying all kinds of free pamphlets and circulars from a local coffee house. Mr. Adams immediately asks Mr. Mark why the class went to that coffee house during the lunch break. When he hears Mr. Mark's answer, he is delighted: (Average rigor) *(Skill 2.5)*

A) Mr. Mark says they went looking for environmental print and words with a café and latte root.

B) Mr. Mark says they didn't spend any money and got free hot chocolate.

C) The children will have to summarize a pamphlet as homework.

D) All of the above.

54. Prioritize these individuals in terms of their contributions regarding young children; intermediate-aged, middle level children; and all children, respectively. (Rigorous) *(Skill 2.6)*

A) Randolph Caldecott, E.D. Hirsch, John Newbery.

B) Randolph Caldecott, John Newbery, E.D. Hirsch.

C) John Newbery, E.D. Hirsch, Randolph Caldecott.

D) E.D. Hirsch, Randolph Caldecott, John Newbery.

55. _____ is to the Stanford Achievement Test as_____ is to the Metropolitan Achievement Test. (Rigorous) *(Skill 2.6)*

   A) Predictive; diagnostic.

   B) Individual; group.

   C) Criterion-referenced; norm referenced.

   D) Written; oral.

56. Is it easier for ELL students who read in their first language to learn to read in English? (Rigorous) *(Skill 2.6)*

   A) No, because the letter-sound relationships in English are unique.

   B) Yes, because this will give the children confidence.

   C) No, because there is often interference from one language to the next.

   D) Yes, because the process is the same regardless of the language.

57. The teacher is watching the children go from oral speech into writing. The teacher says, "Great job:" The children are demonstrating: (Easy) *(Skill 2.6)*

   A) A good decoding.

   B) A good recoding.

   C) A good encoding.

   D) A good coding.

58. As part of study about the agricultural products of their state, children have identified 22 different types of apples produced in the state. They can use a _____to compare and contrast these different types of apples: (Rigorous) *(Skill 2.6)*

   A) Word web.

   B) Semantic map.

   C) Semantic features analysis grid.

   D) All of the above.

59. One of the many ways in which a child can demonstrate comprehension of a story is by: (Average rigor) *(Skill 2.6)*

   A) Filling in a strategy sheet.

   B) Retelling the story orally.

   C) Retelling the story in writing.

   D) All of the above.

60. "Sounds right" can sound wrong to: (Average rigor) *(Skill 2.6)*

   A) Any reader who is not a fluent or early reader.

   B) AN ELL reader.

   C) A struggling reader.

   D) None of the above.

61. Making inferences from the text means that the reader: (Average rigor) *(Skill 2.6)*

   A) Is making informed judgments based on available evidence.

   B) Is making a guess based on prior experiences.

   C) Is making a guess based on what the reader would like to be true of the text.

   D) All of the above.

62. Mr. Anders is a brand new teacher who is not from the neighborhood where his school is located. He is a bit nervous as this is his first teaching assignment. He does not yet know how to relax enough to get his students to activate prior experience. He should: (Rigorous) *(Skill 2.6)*

   A) Try a free recall question: Tell us what you know about...

   B) Try an unstructured Question: Let's talk about...

   C) Use word association: What do you associate X with?

   D) All of the above.

63. The best literary strategy that a teacher can use to activate prior knowledge is: (Average rigor) *(Skill 2.6)*

   A) Predicting and previewing a story.

   B) Story mapping.

   C) Venn diagramming.

   D) Linear arrays.

64. Ms. Angel has to be certain that her fourth graders know the characteristics of the historical fiction genre. She can best support them in becoming comfortable with this genre by: (Average rigor) *(Skill 2.6)*

   A) Providing sequel and prequel writing opportunities using that genre.

   B) Reading them many different works from that genre.

   C) A and B.

   D) Having them look up the definition of that genre in a literary encyclopedia.

65. A character who changes during a story is called _____, while a character who is one-dimensional is called _____.
(Rigorous) *(Skill 2.6)*

A) Dynamite; stereotyped.

B) Motivated; unmotivated.

C) Dynamic; flat.

D) The protagonist; the antagonist.

66. In the following sentence, identify the underlined words: "The tourniquet was <u>wound</u> around the <u>wound</u>." (Rigorous) *(Skill 2.6)*

A) Homophones.

B) Homodicts.

C) Homonyms.

D) Homographs.

67. Bill has been called up to the teacher for an individual conference. She asks him to retell one of the books he has listed on his weekly log. He begins and is still talking 7 minutes later. Most probably, Bill: (Easy) *(Skill 2.6)*

A) Told the entire story with all its details and minor characters.

B) May or may not have really gotten the main points and perspectives of the story.

C) May have really liked the story.

D) None of the above.

68. Vocabulary should be introduced after reading if: (Average rigor) *(Skill 2.6)*

A) The children have identified words from their reading which were difficult and which they need explained.

B) The text is appropriate for vocabulary building.

C) The teacher would like to teach vocabulary after the reading.

D) A and B.

69. The Stop and Think Strategy means that the child reader will: (Average rigor) *(Skill 2.6)*

A) Read through until the end of the story or text.

B) Ask himself or herself if what he or she has read makes sense to him or her.

C) Stop after reading some text and write down his/her concerns.

D) All of the above.

70. Cause-and-effect is to _____ as chronological is to ____. (Rigorous) *(Skill 2.7)*

A) Nonfiction; fiction.

B) Text structure; story.

C) Comprehension; appreciation.

D) Writing; reading.

71. While the supervisor is pleased overall with Barbara's first year of teaching, he feels that given the fact that two of her students are transfers from Mexico and one student has a hearing impairment, she has to plan for: (Rigorous) *(Skill 2.7)*

A) Extra homework for all of them.

B) Extra time for the hearing impaired child.

C) A buddy to work with the two students from Mexico.

D) Differentiated instruction to meet these students' varied special needs.

72. It is likely one could use the newspaper to teach all of the following except: (Easy) *(Skill 2.7)*

A) Functional reading.

B) Lifelong reading.

C) Reading charts and graphs.

D) Literary criticism.

73. Ms. Ramirez also wants the children to share their functional reading skills with their families, so she asks that they take the newspapers home to focus on the: (Average rigor) *(Skill 2.7)*

A) Advice columns.

B) Fill in coupons.

C) Metropolitan news briefs.

D) Weather section.

74. Mr. Bedner was pleased with Ms. Neilson's reading lesson, but he realized that she would have visually represented the comparisons she was trying to get the children to make better, if she had used: (Average rigor) *(Skill 2.7)*

A) A big book.

B) More expressive language.

C) A better literary example.

D) A graphic organizer.

75. When taking a child's running record, the kinds of self corrections the child makes: (Average rigor) *(Skill 3.8)*

A) Are not important, but the percentage of accuracy is important.

B) May show something about which cueing systems the child relies on.

C) Can be meaningful if analyzed over several records.

D) Both B and C.

76. The reliability of standardized test is measured by: (Rigorous) *(Skill 3.8)*

A) The percentage of children scoring in a bell-shaped curve.

B) Its lack of bias.

C) Whether it tests what it is supposed to test.

D) Its consistency over time.

77. A quartile on a test is: (Average rigor) *(Skill 3.8)*

A) A quarter of the grades grouped.

B) The division of the percentiles into four segments each of which is called a quartile.

C) 25 of the tests scored.

D) B and C.

78. Validity in assessment means: (Easy) *(Skill 3.8)*

A) The test went off without any previewing of the questions or leaks on its contents.

B) The majority of test takers passed.

C) The correct time was allowed for the children to complete the test.

D) The test assessed what it was supposed to assess and measure.

79. "Bias" in testing occurs when: (Average rigor) *(Skill 3.8)*

A) The assessment instrument is not an objective, fair and impartial one for a given cultural, ethnic, or special need participant.

B) The testing administrator is biased.

C) The same test is given with no time considerations or provisions for those in need of more time or those who have handicapping conditions.

D) All of the above.

80. **Norm-referenced tests: (Rigorous)** *(Skill 3.8)*

A) Give information only about the local samples results.

B) Provide information about the local test takers did compared to a representative sampling of national test takers.

C) Make no comparisons to national test takers.

D) None of the above.

81. **If you get your raw score on a test, you will get: (Easy)** *(Skill 3.8)*

A) The actual number of points you scored on the test.

B) The percentage score of the number of questions you answered correctly.

C) A letter grade for your work on the test.

D) An aggregated score for your performance on the text.

82. **The data coordinator of the district who is concerned with federal funding for reading will probably want to start aggregating scores immediately because: (Rigorous)** *(Skill 3.8)*

A) The public has a right to know.

B) By aggregating, the individual scores can be combined to view performance trends across groups.

C) This will help the district determine which groups need more remedial instruction.

D) B and C.

83. **A standardized test will be: (Easy)** *(Skill 3.8)*

A) Given out with the same predetermined questions and format to all.

B) Not be given to certain children.

C) If given out in exactly the same format with the same content, may be taken over a lengthier test period (i.e. 4 hours instead of three or two).

D) All of the above.

84. Ms. Payne is preparing for a parent teacher conference. She does all of the following EXCEPT: (Easy) *(Skill 3.9)*

A) Collects individual child running records.

B) Puts away all the book bags and leveled pots so the classroom will be more spacious.

C) Puts out by each child's seat the child's weekly log and spelling folder.

D) Sets up work samples by each child's place.

85. In terms of a balanced literacy classroom, a "leveled bin" indicates: (Easy) *(Skill 3.9)*

A) A bin of paperback books set at the child's eye level for reading choices.

B) A bin with books the child has selected for him- or herself.

C) A bin with books leveled by the teacher.

D) A bin with different reading materials, including magazines, at a child's level.

86. Mr. Matthews has been told that he will have to support some special needs readers in his classroom in addition to the rest of the students. He can expect to have: (Easy) (Skill 3.9)

A) Gifted children who are accelerated in reading skills for their grade and age.

B) Children who have disabilities and will need special support in accessing the content and methods he uses with the rest of the class.

C) Children who come from native language backgrounds other than English.

D) Children who display the capacities and needs detailed in A and B.

87. A "decodable text" is: (Easy) *(Skill 3.9)*

A) A text that a child can read aloud with correct pronunciations.

B) A text that a child can answer comprehension questions about with a high percentage of accuracy.

C) Text written to match the sequence of letter-sound relationships that have been taught.

D) None of the above.

88. **Emergent literacy is: (Rigorous) *(Skill 3.9)***

   A) An updated term for reading readiness.

   B) A stage that follows early reading.

   C) A description of children's gradual entry into reading from birth onward.

   D) A set of incremental skills that must be mastered before reading.

89. **As far as the balanced literacy movement is concerned the "WHOLE" is: (Average rigor) *(Skill 3.9)***

   A) All the reading themes to be covered that day.

   B) The whole class meeting for the mini lesson.

   C) The complete unit to be covered over the month.

   D) All of the reading and writing work to be done in connection with one book.

90. **As part of a study for a unit on the history of Massachusetts, Mr. Gentry is using the early childhood book *26 Letters and 99 Cents* by Tina Hoban. He wants his readers to study it and create a more detailed guide to their state using its concept. This is a technique frequently used in: (Average rigor) *(Skill 3.9)***

   A) Reading and writing workshop.

   B) Writing process instruction.

   C) Readers workshop.

   D) Technical writing.

91. **A teacher is asking children to look at the beginning letters of words. She then asks the child to connect the beginning letter to the text and story and to think about what word would make sense there. This is an example of: (Average rigor) *(Skill 3.9)***

   A) A balanced literacy approach.

   B) A phonemic approach.

   C) A phonics approach.

   D) AN ELL differentiated approach.

92. By November the first graders have a vocabulary of words which they can correctly pronounce and read aloud. These words are their: (Rigorous) *(Skill 3.9)*

    A) Sight vocabulary.

    B) Recognition vocabulary.

    C) Personal vocabulary.

    D) Working vocabulary.

93. When teaching children to read nonfiction, the knowledge of different text structures will provide them with: (Rigorous) *(Skill 3.9)*

    A) Predictable questions for self-correction.

    B) The fluency to promote reading speed.

    C) Skills to navigate different parts of the book

    D) Schemata that promote comprehension.

94. In the balanced literacy approach, ability groups are: (Rigorous) *(Skill 3.9)*

    A) Abolished.

    B) Recommended.

    C) Mixed.

    D) Changeable.

95. What is the optimum order for teaching these phonics skills? (Rigorous) *(3.9)*

    A) Long vowels, digraphs and blends, diphthongs, short vowels, and r-controlled words.

    B) Short vowels, long vowels, digraphs and blends, diphthongs, and r-controlled words.

    C) Digraphs and blends, diphthongs, long vowels, short vowels, and r-controlled words.

    D) Short vowels, digraphs and blends, long vowels, diphthongs, and r-controlled words.

96. The strongest purpose of an author's chair is to: (Rigorous) *(Skill 3.9)*

    A) Give recognition to children as authors.

    B) Allow the children to hear a variety of readers.

    C) Give volunteers an opportunity to read.

    D) Give the children practice in oral expressiveness.

97. All of the following can be added to a root word except: (Rigorous) *(Skill 3.9)*

A) An affix.

B) An inflectional ending.

C) A compound word.

D) A prefix.

98. A veteran teacher waited for her adult daughter outside of her daughter's first class in the Teaching of Reading. As she and her daughter talked about the first session of the course, the teacher never heard an explicit mention of the teaching of reading. All she heard about was: (Easy) *(Skill 3.9)*

A) Learning about narratives.

B) Dealing with text structures.

C) Constructing meaning.

D) All of the above.

99. A very bright child in a grade one class came from a family which did not a have a strong oral story telling or story reading tradition in its native language. This child would need support in developing: (Rigorous) *(Skill 3.9)*

A) Letter-sound correspondence skills.

B) Schemata for generic concepts most children have in their memories and experiences based on family oral traditions and read alouds.

C) Oral expressiveness.

D) B and C.

100. Ms. Ancess used to take time to have her children memorize major poems and even had an assembly for parents and school staff where the children dramatically recited various poems. Now that she is worried about the children's reading scores, she doesn't want to waste time with this memorization. However, if she still includes this high interest, child-centered experience: (Rigorous) *(Skill 3.9)*

A) The children can use their oral fluency and her modeling as a bridge for enhanced comprehension.

B) The children can get a sense of "ownership" of the words.

C) The children's memory skills will improve.

D) The children's test scores will probably suffer.

Answer Key

1. C	35. D	69. B
2. D	36. D	70. B
3. C	37. A	71. D
4. B	38. D	72. C
5. C	39. D	73. B
6. D	40. D	74. A
7. B	41. B	75. D
8. C	42. B	76. D
9. B	43. C	77. B
10. C	44. B	78. D
11. B	45. B	79. D
12. D	46. B	80. B
13. D	47. D	81. A
14. B	48. C	82. D
15. B	49. C	83. D
16. C	50. C	84. B
17. C	51. D	85. C
18. C	52. D	86. D
19. C	53. D	87. A
20. B	54. B	88. C
21. D	55. C	89. B
22. B	56. D	90. A
23. B	57. C	91. C
24. A	58. D	92. B
25. C	59. D	93. D
26. A	60. B	94. D
27. C	61. A	95. D
28. C	62. D	96. A
29. C	63. A	97. C
30. D	64. C	98. C
31. D	65. C	99. B
32. C	66. D	100. A
33. C	67. A	
34. D	68. D	

Rigor Table

Easy	1, 14, 15, 22, 26, 32, 45, 47, 57, 67, 72, 78, 83, 84, 85, 86, 87, 98
Average	2, 4, 7, 11, 16, 18, 19, 20, 25, 28, 29, 30, 31, 34, 35, 36, 37, 38, 40, 41, 42, 43, 44, 48, 50, 53, 59, 60, 61, 63, 64, 68, 69, 73, 74, 75, 77, 79, 81, 89, 90, 91
Rigorous	3, 5, 6, 8, 9, 10, 12, 13, 17, 21, 23, 24, 27, 33, 39, 46, 49, 51, 52, 54, 55, 56, 58, 62, 65, 66, 70, 71, 76, 80, 82, 88, 92, 93, 94, 95, 96, 97, 99, 100

Answers with Rationale

1. **The major difference between phonemic and phonological awareness is:** *(Easy) (Skill 1.1)*

    A) One deals with a series of discrete sounds and the other with sound-spelling relationships.

    B) One is involved with teaching and learning alliteration and rhymes.

    C) Phonemic awareness is a specific type of phonological awareness that deals with separate phonemes within a given word.

    D) Phonological awareness is associated with printed words.

    The Answer is C. This is a memorization question. By definition, phonemic awareness falls under the phonological awareness umbrella. All of the other choices do not deal with the DIFFERENCE between the two types of awareness.

2. **Mr. Sanchez is having his students work with one-syllable words, removing the first consonant and substituting another, as in m/ats to h/ats. What reading skill are they working on?** *(Average rigor) (Skill 1.1)*

    A) Morphemic inflections.

    B) Pronouncing short vowels.

    C) Invented spelling.

    D) Phonological awareness.

    The correct answer is "D". While there are inflections ("s") and short vowels)"a") in these words as in Answers "A" and "B," neither is the focus of this activity. These words have standard spellings, not invented as in Answer "C."

3. Most of the children in first-year teacher Ms. James's class are really doing well in their phonemic awareness assessments. However, Ms. James is very concerned about three children who do not seem to be able to distinguish between spoken words that "sound alike," but are different. Since she is a first year teacher, she feels her inexperience may be to blame. In truth, the reason these three children have not yet demonstrated phonemic awareness is most likely that: (Rigorous) (Skill 1.1)

    A) They are not capable of becoming good readers.

    B) They may have problems paying attention.

    C) They may be from an ELL background.

    D) Ms. James does not pronounce the different phonemes clearly enough.

Choice C is correct. The most likely reason that these three children (a minority of the class) are struggling is because they have an ELL background.

4. Gracie seems to be struggling with her reading, even in first grade, although her mother works at a publishing firm and her dad is an editor. Her speech is also full of mispronunciations, although her parents were born in the school neighborhood. Gracie should be checked by: (Average rigor) *(Skill 1.1)*

    A) A reading specialist.

    B) A speech therapist or an audiologist

    C) A pediatrician.

    D) A psychologist.

The correct answer is "B" because Gracie is a neighborhood child and shouldn't be having these difficulties with pronunciation.

5. **Ronald's parents are hearing-impaired. What work will this first grader need most? (Rigorous) *(Skill 1.1)***

    A) Picture cues to promote visual acuity.

    B) Sight word mastery to promote fluency.

    C) Rhymes and read alouds to promote phonological awareness.

    D) Letter-sound practice to promote the alphabetic principle.

The correct answer is "C." Because Ronald's parents either use sign language and/or have compromised articulation, he needs work most on tuning his ear to letter sounds.

6. **The most important reason to keep ongoing assessments of children's phonological awareness is: (Rigorous) *(Skill 1.1)***

    A) To be accountable to the principal.

    B) To compare with teachers of the same grade level.

    C) To have data for report cards.

    D) To plan curriculum.

The correct answer is "D." Ongoing assessments allow the teacher to adjust and plan to meet the needs of the students in the classroom.

7. **A stationery store owner in the neighborhood of the school is amused by the fact that the children on a school walk, are rushing up to various store signs and street signs. The children are probably exploring: (Average rigor) (Skill 1.1)**

    A) The alphabetic principle.

    B) The principle that print carries meaning.

    C) Letter sound recognition.

    D) Phonemic awareness.

The behavior described here only matches one reading activity, **"B."**

8. **Clapping is the best way to learn syllable divisions because:** (Rigorous) *(Skill 1.1)*

   A) Children enjoy the activity and are motivated to learn.

   B) Syllables are rhythmic.

   C) The activity is both auditory and kinesthetic.

   D) Movement aids memory.

The correct answer is "C." Learning supported by two modalities is always stronger than only one.

9. **Arrange these phenomena in the order in which they are mastered by children in reading:** (Rigorous) *(Skill 1.2)*

   A) Environmental print, alphabetic principle, phonological awareness, decoding.

   B) Environmental print, phonological awareness, alphabetic principle, decoding.

   C) Environmental print, decoding, alphabetic principle, phonological awareness.

   D) Environmental print, phonological awareness, decoding, alphabetic principle.

The correct answer is "B." First, children notice print on signs, billboards, restaurants, and the like. Next they become aware of the sounds of language and are able to manipulate them, as in rhymes. Third, they realize that particular sounds match certain letters and letter combinations, and finally, they crack the code and "unlock" words through correct letter-sound correspondences.

10. **The value of allowing children to use invented spelling?** (Rigorous) *(Skill 1.2)*

    A) It frees up the teacher to get around to many children during Writing Workshop.

    B) It ultimately contributes to good spelling skills.

    C) It helps children listen to the sounds of words they are attempting to write.

    D) It makes children feel proud of their writing.

The correct answer is "C." When creating their own temporary invented spellings, children listen carefully and encode sounds sequentially in words. This lays a foundation for later phonics learning.

11. **It is 4 PM, yet Francine is still in her classroom. The seats in her classroom are filled with adults of various ages who are holding books. They are seated two by two with both holding copies of the same book. Francine probably is: (Average rigor)** *(Skill 1.2)*

A) Explaining to parents how she will teach a particular story.

B) Demonstrating shared reading with a buddy for volunteer parents.

C) Hosting a parents' organization meeting for her grade level.

D) Distributing old books from the class library to parents.

The answer is "B" because the question details that the adults are seated two by two holding copies of the same book. This is the buddy reading style.

12. **Chard and Osborn (1999) found that children with reading disabilities need to learn the alphabetic principle because: (Rigorous) (Skill 1.2)**

A) The alphabet has predictable letter-sound relationships.

B) Learning sight words is harder for the disabled reader.

C) Knowing the alphabet will give these readers confidence.

D) The relationship between letters and sounds is central to early reading.

The correct answer is "D." The most important concept of learning here is letter-sound relationships.

13. _____**is to letter-sound relationships as ___is to word meanings. (Rigorous)** *(Skill 1.2)*

A) Decoding; syntax.

B) Phonological awareness; phonemic awareness.

C) Syntax; semantics.

D) Graphophonemic awareness; semantics.

The correct answer is "D." The relationship is this analogy is one of terms to definitions.

14.   **The purpose of taking dictation is to:** (Easy) *(Skill 1.2)*

    A) Demonstrate how to copy down speech.

    B) Make a connection and promote awareness of the relationship between spoken and written language.

    C) Authenticate the children's comments.

    D) Raise the children's self-esteem.

The correct answer is "B." By watching what the teacher is doing, children learn that what they say can be written down. This insight is a major breakthrough in reading and writing.

15.   **To encode means that you:** (Easy) *(Skill 1.2)*

    A) Decode a second time.

    B) Construct meaning from a code.

    C) Tell someone a message.

    D) None of the above.

The answer is "B" and is a definition question. To encode means to construct meaning from a code.

16. **Once a teacher has carefully recorded and documented a running record: (Average rigor)** *(Skill 1.2)*

A) There is nothing further to do as long as the teacher keeps the running record for conferences and documentation of grades.

B) The teacher should review the running record and other subsequent ones taken for growth over time.

C) The teacher should differentiate instruction for that particular student as indicated by growth over time and evidence of other needs.

D) Both B and C.

Students learn at different rates, therefore students in any class will be at varying levels of learning. By differentiating instruction and incorporating assessment **for** learning rather than assessment **of** learning, teachers can help students succeed. When teachers assess student growth over time and monitor the areas in which they are experiencing difficulty, they can alter the instruction and the activities to match student needs. **The answer is "C."**

17. **Rudolf Flesch is to____as Marie Clay is to_____.** (Rigorous) (Skill 1.3)

A) Cultural literacy; balanced literacy.

B) Decodable books; leveled books.

C) Phonics; Reading Recovery.

D) Wordless picture books; picture story books.

The correct answer is "C." This analogy expresses the relationship of association.

18. **Cues in reading are:** (Average rigor) *(Skill 1.3)*

    A) Vowel sounds.

    B) Digraphs.

    C) Sources of information used by readers to help them construct meaning.

    D) Tips given by the teacher.

This is a definition question and the **answer is "C."**

19. **Asking a child if what he or she has read makes sense to him or her prompts the child to use:** (Average rigor) *(Skill 1.3)*

    A) Phonics cues.

    B) Syntactic cues.

    C) Semantic cues.

    D) Prior knowledge.

Semantic cues are the hints that students can discern from the reading to help them make sense of the text. In some cases, the message of the text depends on the other words around them, so students learn how to determine the meaning from context clues. **The answer must be "C."**

20. **When they are in 6th grade, children should be able to independently go through an unfamiliar collection and:** (Average rigor) *(Skill 1.3)*

    A) Use only the table of contents.

    B) Use the first line indices, and find a poem by author and subject.

    C) Use only the glossary.

    D) Read bar graphs but not pie charts.

The correct answer is "B." This choice is an appropriate task for a sixth grade learner.

21. **One of the most important features in nonfiction books that children should learn to read includes:** (Rigorous) *(Skill 1.3)*

   A) Page numbers.

   B) Picture cues.

   C) Characterization.

   D) Captions.

The correct answer is "D." Children should know page numbers as soon as they begin to read.

22. **As the visitors from the United Kingdom tour the school, they are pleased to hear a sing-song chant "Don't fall asleep at the page, don't forget the _____"** Mr. Adams explains to them that the first graders are learning about pointing at words and moving from the left to the right. This is called: (Easy) *(Skill 1.3)*

   A) Directionality.

   B) Return sweep.

   C) Top to bottom.

   D) Line for line reading.

The answer is "B" and this term is in the Glossary.

23. **Environmental print is available in all of the following except:** (Rigorous) *(Skill 1.3)*

   A) Within a newspaper.

   B) On the page of a library book.

   C) On a supermarket circular.

   D) In a commercial flyer.

The key word here is "EXCEPT" and environmental print is not defined as print in a library book, **so choice "B" is the right one.**

24. **Children learn book- handling skills best through:** (Rigorous) *(Skill 1.3)*

A) Teacher modeling during shared reading.

B) Parents reading to their children at home.

C) Imitation of book buddies or peer tutors from another class.

D) Direct instruction by the teacher.

The correct answer is "A." Children will pick up book handling skills from watching the teacher's handling of Big Books as well as regular-sized books during read alouds. Teachers consciously draw children's attention to the book's features, such as orienting the book, the front and back cover, the title page, and the like.

25. **The best way for a primary grade teacher to model directionality and one to one word matching would be:** (Average rigor) *(Skill 1.3)*

A) Using a regular library or classroom text book.

B) Using her own personal reading book.

C) Using a big book.

D) Using a book dummy.

Key word in this question is "best" and **the answer is "C"** because this type of a book is best for teaching and display.

26. **To decode is to:** (Easy) (Skill 1.3)

A) Construct meaning

B) Sound out a printed sequence of letters.

C) Use a special code to decipher a message.

D) Write out what one hears.

"A" is the correct answer. Decoding is constructing meaning.

27. **By definition, which children in a classroom will have trouble with syntactic cues? (Rigorous) *(Skill 1.3)***

    A) Those from families who do not have household libraries.

    B) Those not in a top reading group.

    C) Those from ELL backgrounds.

    D) All of the above.

This question can actually only have a single correct answer. **It is "C"** because by definition a child from an ELL background does not have a strong accurate sense of what "sounds right" in English.

28. **A natural role for a highly proficient reader would be: (Average rigor) *(Skill 1.3)***

    A) To assist the teacher with cleaning the classroom and organizing the student folders.

    B) To develop charts for the teacher by copying needed poems for full class study.

    C) Tutor and support struggling readers.

    D) Work on his/her own interests while the teacher works with the rest of the class.

While all of the choices are possibilities, the concept of the highly proficient reader tutoring leads to **answer "C."**

29. **Based on individual conferences with many children, the teacher realizes that although they are all self-improving readers, they need help in better use of the context to define words. The teacher decided to try the use of: (Average rigor) *(Skill 1.3)***

    A) A dictionary to look up words.

    B) A thesaurus to use with the dictionary.

    C) Contextual redefinition training.

    D) Instruction in how to effectively use a dictionary.

The answer is "C" and the trick is to notice the "better use of context" in the question and match it up with "C," contextual redefinition training.

30. To promote word study, children can: (Average rigor) *(Skill 1.4)*

A) Be required to go to the dictionary at least once or twice a day.

B) Collect and share words of interest they find in their readings.

C) Do vocabulary work sheets from a basal reader or commercial vocabulary book.

D) Do all of the above.

All of the answers will promote vocabulary, **so the answer is "D."**

31. In order to get children to compile specialized vocabulary, they can use: (Average rigor) *(Skill 1.4)*

A) Newspapers.

B) Internet resources and approved web-sites that focus on their special interest.

C) Experts they can interview.

D) All of the above.

The answer is "D" because all of the responses are correct.

32. Teachers should select at least _____words for pre-reading vocabulary discussion: (Easy) *(Skill 1.4)*

A) 12.

B) 15.

C) 2-3.

D) 8-10.

The correct answer is "C," 2-3 words. Teachers should select a small number of words for pre-teaching to allow the students time to comprehend the text and achieve the objectives related to the reading. For example, in a non-fiction text, these words could be key terms related to the main topic. Even students with an extensive oral vocabulary may not be able to recognize words in print because they are not words that they normally encounter in their reading. The activities the teacher plans in relation to the words will help the students internalize the strategies more readily when only a few words are selected each time.

33. The word "bat" is a __word for "batter-up": (Rigorous) *(Skill 1.4)*

   A) Suffix.

   B) Prefix.

   C) Root word.

   D) Inflectional ending.

The answer is "C." This is an example of a root.

34. An effective way to build vocabulary and to make connections with mandated science and mathematics material is to teach Greek and Latin roots using: (Average rigor) *(Skill 1.4)*

   A) Semantic maps.

   B) Hierarchical arrays.

   C) Linear arrays.

   D) Word webs.

The answer is "D" and historically these have been used to teach Greek and Latin roots.

35. To help children with "main idea" questions, the teacher should: (Average rigor) *(Skill 1.4)*

   A) Give out a strategy sheet on the main idea for children to place their reader's notebooks.

   B) Model responding to such a question as part of guided reading.

   C) Have children create "main idea questions" to go with their writing.

   D) All of the above.

The correct answer is "D." All three options will assist children with identifying the main idea of a selection.

36. **Dictionary study: (Average rigor)** *(Skill 1.4)*

    A) Can begin in grades 1 or 2.

    B) Can begin in pre-K using the lush picture dictionaries.

    C) Should start on grade three level.

    D) A and B.

Choice "D" is correct. Young learners are able to and should utilize dictionary skills.

37. **An excellent research project that can combine dictionary study with science research would be: (Average rigor)** *(Skill 1.4)*

    A) A student-authored dictionary with terms and phrases about earthworms.

    B) A teacher developed specialized dictionary of words and phrases about earthworms.

    C) A collection of articles on earthworms put together by the school librarian.

    D) B and C.

Choice "A", which deals with a student product, is correct. The others are all adult-centered.

38. **Mr. Adams has complained to Mr. Mark that there are too many newspapers piled up in his classroom. Mr. Mark has responded that he does not want to throw away these piled up newspapers because: (Average rigor)** *(Skill 1.4)*

    A) They can be used for letter –sound correspondence.

    B) They represent environmental print.

    C) They can be used to create print-meaning signs.

    D) All of the above.

This is a question where choice "D" makes good sense to a teacher who knows the value of having newspapers for class projects.

39. Sometimes children can be asked to demonstrate their understanding of a text in a non-written format. This might include all of the following except: (Rigorous) (Skill 2.5)

   A) A story map.

   B) A Venn diagram.

   C) Storyboarding a part of the story with dialogue bubbles.

   D) Retelling or paraphrasing.

Answer "D" is correct. Retelling and paraphrasing can be in oral form whereas the other choices all involve writing or the use of pencil and paper. By asking students to retell a story, the teacher can determine the level of comprehension. Of course, this has to be modeled for the student, especially paraphrasing, so that the student relates the important facts or events and does not include any information that is not necessary.

40. The concerned parent whose child had a visual impairment wanted as much help for him as the teacher and the school district could give her. She begged: "Please, he didn't attend pre-school, he has no prior knowledge. Strictly speaking this is: (Average rigor) (Skill 2.5)

   A) Correct, since he didn't get pre-school experiences.

   B) Incorrect, since prior knowledge covers everyone's experiences.

   C) Incorrect, since he did have prior knowledge experiences but these didn't match those of many of his peers, so he would need to enhance his prior knowledge.

   D) B and C.

The correct choice is "D." All individuals have some background with prior knowledge.

41. Randy is proud of how many new vocabulary words he has learned. He enjoys playing with a device his teacher has, since it helps him to show all the words he can create from various letters. The device is a: (Average rigor) *(Skill 2.5)*

    A) Word strip.

    B) Letter holder for making words.

    C) Word mask.

    D) Computer.

The answer is "B" and this is a familiar device in today's reading classroom.

42. "Beautiful Beth is the Best Girl in the Bradley Bay area." This sentence could be used to help children learn about: (Average rigor) *(Skill 2.5)*

    A) Assonance.

    B) Alliteration.

    C) Rhyming pairs.

    D) None of the above.

This is a question that any English literature or Reading major can answer. **The answer is "B."**

43. A district observer notes that fifth graders are showing younger peers in the third grade how to hold a book and walk around with it, they assume: (Average rigor) *(Skill 2.5)*

    A) That the fifth graders are particularly theatrical.

    B) That the fifth graders are proud of how they read stories aloud.

    C) That the fifth graders are training the younger children in book holding.

    D) That this has nothing to do with instruction.

This is a standard part of "book holding," **so that the answer is "C."**

44. When you ask a child if what he or she has just read "sounds right" to him or her, you are trying to get that child to use: (Average rigor) *(Skill 2.5)*

    A) Phonics cues.

    B) Syntactic cues.

    C) Semantic cues.

    D) Prior knowledge.

This is another one of those answers using the language of linguistics in reading. **The answer has to be "B,"** syntactic clues.

45. Children "own" words when all of the following happen except: (Easy) *(Skill 2.5)*

    A) They find these words on their own.

    B) The teacher provides a mandated word list.

    C) They use the words in their own writings.

    D) The words appear in literature that interests them.

Choice "B" is the correct answer. Children do not own words when the teacher puts up a mandated word list.

46. Pre-teaching vocabulary is to_____as choral reading is to _____. (Rigorous) (Skill 2.5)

    A) Comprehension; letter-sound relationships.

    B) Fluency; articulation.

    C) Esthetic appreciation; comprehension.

    D) Comprehension; fluency.

The correct answer is "B." Pre-teaching vocabulary is to fluency as choral reading is to articulation.

47. **Before selecting words for study, a teacher might:** (Easy) *(Skill 2.5)*

A) Read the story and complete story mapping.

B) Ask advice from a veteran teacher and the grade leader.

C) Look in a teacher's guide and choose important concepts listed there.

D) All of the above are correct

Choice "D" is the correct answer. All three options are useful methods a teacher might utilize.

48. **A teacher discovers after considering his class's prior knowledge of the story material that he would need to teach 12 words at least before he starts teaching the story to the whole group. This indicates:** (Average rigor) *(Skill 2.5)*

A) The children will need a read-aloud.

B) The children will need independent reading.

C) The children will need guided reading.

D) The children will need shared reading.

The correct choice is "C." Generally during read-aloud you do not stop to explain many words. You would not want to give material for independent or shared reading where so many words had to be explained.

49. The teacher is working on a life science unit in grade five and using many print and electronic sources for information. Some of the words in the unit have a serial and others a categorical relationship to one another. To help the children's comprehension, the teacher could now: (Rigorous) (Skill 2.5)

A) Use a root family diagram or tree.

B) Work with base words.

C) Use hierarchical and linear arrays.

D) Create separate semantic maps of each word.

The correct answer is "C." It is the best answer because of the relationships—serial and categorical—among the words the teacher wants the children to tackle.

50. **Direct teaching of a concept or strategy means: (Average rigor)** *(Skill 2.5)*

A) The teacher teaches the concept or strategy as part of a genre lesson.

B) The teacher teaches the concept as part of the writing workshop.

C) The teacher explicitly announces to the class that this strategy will be taught.

D) The teacher teaches the strategy to a small group of children or to an individual child.

The answer is "C" and this is a definition question.

51.   The substitute teacher starts reading aloud the Big Book (which she has never seen before) on the easel. What do you predict will happen? (Rigorous) *(Skill 2.5)*

A) The children will enjoy hearing the book read by another voice.

B) The teacher's unfamiliarity will lead her to ask excellent prediction questions.

C) The teacher will be excited by what she spontaneously discovers in the book.

D) The teacher will not read very expressively nor will she have a clear purpose for reading the book.

The correct answer is "D." Preparation is key, and is the best way to fully utilize the Big Book lesson in a classroom. In this manner, a teacher can ask appropriate questions and guide the lesson in the manner he or she would like to.

52.   As Ms. Wolmark looks at the mandated vocabulary curriculum for the 6th grade, she notes that she can opt to teach foreign words and abbreviations which have become part of the English language. She decides: (Rigorous) *(Skill 2.5)*

A) To forego that since she is not a teacher of foreign language.

B) To teach only foreign words from the native language of her four ELL students.

C) To use the ELL students' native languages as a start for an extensive study of foreign language words.

D) To teach a minimal number of foreign language words that are now in English.

The correct answer is "D."

53. As Mr. Adams exits the school building, he notices that Mr. Mark, a new teacher, is leading a group of happy-looking fifth graders back into the building. They are carrying all kinds of free pamphlets and circulars from a local coffee house. Mr. Adams immediately asks Mr. Mark why the class went to that coffee house during the lunch break. When he hears Mr. Mark's answer, he is delighted: (Average rigor) *(Skill 2.5)*

   A) Mr. Mark says they went looking for environmental print and words with a café and latte root.

   B) Mr. Mark says they didn't spend any money and got free hot chocolate.

   C) The children will have to summarize a pamphlet as homework.

   D) All of the above.

This is a question where **the correct choice is "D"** and makes good teaching and learning sense.

54. Prioritize these individuals in terms of their contributions regarding young children; intermediate-aged, middle level children; and all children, respectively. (Rigorous) *(Skill 2.6)*

   A) Randolph Caldecott, E.D. Hirsch, John Newbery.

   B) Randolph Caldecott, John Newbery, E.D. Hirsch.

   C) John Newbery, E.D. Hirsch, Randolph Caldecott.

   D) E.D. Hirsch, Randolph Caldecott, John Newbery.

The correct answer is "B." Randolph Caldecott gave his name to the medal given yearly to the best-illustrated picture book for young children; John Newbery's *name* is given to the yearly medal for the best book written for intermediate-middle-level children. E.D. Hirsch conceived of "cultural literacy," which is a set of ideas considered critical for children's, adolescents' and adults' reading comprehension.

55. _____ is to the Stanford Achievement Test as _____ is to the Metropolitan Achievement Test. (Rigorous) *(Skill 2.6)*

    A) Predictive; diagnostic.

    B) Individual; group.

    C) Criterion-referenced; norm referenced.

    D) Written; oral.

The correct answer is "C." Both are written group tests, climinating Answers "B" and "D."

56. Is it easier for ELL students who read in their first language to learn to read in English? (Rigorous) *(Skill 2.6)*

    A) No, because the letter-sound relationships in English are unique.

    B) Yes, because this will give the children confidence.

    C) No, because there is often interference from one language to the next.

    D) Yes, because the process is the same regardless of the language.

The correct answer is "D." The process is the same, regardless of the language.

57. The teacher is watching the children go from oral speech into writing. The teacher says, "Great job:" The children are demonstrating: (Easy) *(Skill 2.6)*

    A) A good decoding.

    B) A good recoding.

    C) A good encoding.

    D) A good coding.

The correct answer is "C." Encoding is what occurs when you recall information and can write it down.

58. As part of study about the agricultural products of their state, children have identified 22 different types of apples produced in the state. They can use a _____ to compare and contrast these different types of apples: (Rigorous) *(Skill 2.6)*

   A) Word web.

   B) Semantic map.

   C) Semantic features analysis grid.

   D) All of the above.

Answer "D" is correct. All of the graphic organizers will help students analyze characteristics of apples that they can then choose from to construct a comparison and contrast paragraph or paper.

59. One of the many ways in which a child can demonstrate comprehension of a story is by: (Average rigor) *(Skill 2.6)*

   A) Filling in a strategy sheet.

   B) Retelling the story orally.

   C) Retelling the story in writing.

   D) All of the above.

The answer is "D" since all the options are good ones.

60. "Sounds right" can sound wrong to: (Average rigor) *(Skill 2.6)*

   A) Any reader who is not a fluent or early reader.

   B) AN ELL reader.

   C) A struggling reader.

   D) None of the above.

This is a truism of ELL education and **the answer is "B."**

61.   **Making inferences from the text means that the reader:** (Average rigor) *(Skill 2.6)*

   A) Is making informed judgments based on available evidence.

   B) Is making a guess based on prior experiences.

   C) Is making a guess based on what the reader would like to be true of the text.

   D) All of the above.

This is a definition question that a literate test taker can answer based on the general definition of inferences. **The answer is "A."**

62.   **Mr. Anders is a brand new teacher who is not from the neighborhood where his school is located. He is a bit nervous as this is his first teaching assignment. He does not yet know how to relax enough to get his students to activate prior experience. He should:** (Rigorous) *(Skill 2.6)*

   A) Try a free recall question: Tell us what you know about...

   B) Try an unstructured Question: Let's talk about...

   C) Use word association: What do you associate X with?

   D) All of the above.

Again this is a common sense question and **"D" is the correct choice**.

63.   **The best literary strategy that a teacher can use to activate prior knowledge is:** (Average rigor) *(Skill 2.6)*

   A) Predicting and previewing a story.

   B) Story mapping.

   C) Venn diagramming.

   D) Linear arrays.

This is a question that a literate test taker could answer and **the best choice is "A"** because in their predictions, children evidence prior knowledge.

64. **Ms. Angel has to be certain that her fourth graders know the characteristics of the historical fiction genre. She can best support them in becoming comfortable with this genre by:** (Average rigor) *(Skill 2.6)*

A) Providing sequel and prequel writing opportunities using that genre.

B) Reading them many different works from that genre.

C) A and B.

D) Having them look up the definition of that genre in a literary encyclopedia.

The answer is "C." Online encyclopedias meet the information technology outcomes that align with language arts outcomes. When students are taught to avail of the online encyclopedias, it can save enormous amounts of space in the classroom as well as trips to the library. Students can complete all their work on the computer without having to stop and thumb through a regular encyclopedia to find the information they need.

65. **A character who changes during a story is called _____, while a character who is one-dimensional is called ____.**
(Rigorous) *(Skill 2.6)*

A) Dynamite; stereotyped.

B) Motivated; unmotivated.

C) Dynamic; flat.

D) The protagonist; the antagonist.

The correct answer is "C."

66. In the following sentence, identify the underlined words: "The tourniquet was <u>wound</u> around the <u>wound</u>." (Rigorous) *(Skill 2.6)*

   A) Homophones.

   B) Homodicts.

   C) Homonyms.

   D) Homographs.

The correct answer is "D." Homographs are spelled the same but pronounced differently and have different meanings, such as lead and lead. Homophones (Answer "A) are the same as homonyms (Answer "C) _. They sound the same but have different spellings such as red and read. Homodicts (Answer "B) do not exist.

67. Bill has been called up to the teacher for an individual conference. She asks him to retell one of the books he has listed on his weekly log. He begins and is still talking 7 minutes later. Most probably, Bill: (Easy) *(Skill 2.6)*

   A) Told the entire story with all its details and minor characters.

   B) May or may not have really gotten the main points and perspectives of the story.

   C) May have really liked the story.

   D) None of the above.

The correct answer is "A." This student most likely presented in a very detailed way, and may need further instruction on pulling the main points from the book for a presentation.

68. **Vocabulary should be introduced after reading if:** (Average rigor) *(Skill 2.6)*

   A) The children have identified words from their reading which were difficult and which they need explained.

   B) The text is appropriate for vocabulary building.

   C) The teacher would like to teach vocabulary after the reading.

   D) A and B.

Answer "D" which includes both "A" and "B" is the right choice.
Vocabulary introduced by children and a good text with opportunities to expand vocabulary are needed.

69. **The Stop and Think Strategy means that the child reader will:** (Average rigor) *(Skill 2.6)*

   A) Read through until the end of the story or text.

   B) Ask himself or herself if what he or she has read makes sense to him or her.

   C) Stop after reading some text and write down his/her concerns.

   D) All of the above

The correct answer is "B." This question requires the very specific definition of the STOP and THINK strategy.

70. Cause-and-effect is to _____ as chronological is to _____.
(Rigorous) *(Skill 2.7)*

   A) Nonfiction; fiction.

   B) Text structure; story.

   C) Comprehension; appreciation.

   D) Writing; reading.

The correct answer is "B." The relationship in this analogy is characteristic-to-thing. Cause-and-effect is one way a text structure is organized; stories are conventionally organized chronologically.

71. While the supervisor is pleased overall with Barbara's first year of teaching, he feels that given the fact that two of her students are transfers from Mexico and one student has a hearing impairment, she has to plan for: (Rigorous) *(Skill 2.7)*

   A) Extra homework for all of them.

   B) Extra time for the hearing impaired child.

   C) A buddy to work with the two students from Mexico.

   D) Differentiated instruction to meet these students' varied special needs.

The correct answer is "D." This choice includes the special approaches Barbara will have to take with her ELL and special needs students.

72. It is likely one could use the newspaper to teach all of the following <u>except</u>: (Easy) *(Skill 2.7)*

   A) Functional reading.

   B) Lifelong reading.

   C) Reading charts and graphs.

   D) Literary criticism.

The answer is "C." Functional literacy refers to knowing things that students have to do on a day to day basis. Reading a recipe is classified as functional literacy because students learn how to read directions to perform a task.

73. Ms. Ramirez also wants the children to share their functional reading skills with their families, so she asks that they take the newspapers home to focus on the: (Average rigor) *(Skill 2.7)*

   A) Advice columns.

   B) Fill in coupons.

   C) Metropolitan news briefs.

   D) Weather section.

The correct answer is "B." Coupons, like want ads are functional the families can fill in or act on.

74. Mr. Bedner was pleased with Ms. Neilson's reading lesson, but he realized that she would have visually represented the comparisons she was trying to get the children to make better, if she had used: (Average rigor) *(Skill 2.7)*

   A) A big book.

   B) More expressive language.

   C) A better literary example.

   D) A graphic organizer.

The answer is "A" because the BIG BOOK is a good visual display tool.

75. **When taking a child's running record, the kinds of self corrections the child makes:** (Average rigor) *(Skill 3.8)*

   A) Are not important, but the percentage of accuracy is important.

   B) May show something about which cueing systems the child relies on.

   C) Can be meaningful if analyzed over several records.

   D) Both B and C.

The answer is "D" and related to taking a child's running record.

76. **The reliability of standardized test is measured by:** (Rigorous) *(Skill 3.8)*

   A) The percentage of children scoring in a bell-shaped curve.

   B) Its lack of bias.

   C) Whether it tests what it is supposed to test.

   D) Its consistency over time.

The correct answer is "D." A test is reliable if a student would achieve the same or a similar score if s/he took the test at two different times.

77. **A quartile on a test is:** (Average rigor) *(Skill 3.8)*

   A) A quarter of the grades grouped.

   B) The division of the percentiles into four segments each of which is called a quartile.

   C) 25 of the tests scored.

   D) B and C.

The correct answer is "B." While this is also a definition question, choice "B" is one that a linguist would choose.

78. **Validity in assessment means:** (Easy) *(Skill 3.8)*

   A) The test went off without any previewing of the questions or leaks on its contents.

   B) The majority of test takers passed.

   C) The correct time was allowed for the children to complete the test.

   D) The test assessed what it was supposed to assess and measure.

The correct answer is "D" and it also makes good sense to the test taker.

79. **"Bias" in testing occurs when:** (Average rigor) *(Skill 3.8)*

   A) The assessment instrument is not an objective, fair and impartial one for a given cultural, ethnic, or special need participant.

   B) The testing administrator is biased.

   C) The same test is given with no time considerations or provisions for those in need of more time or those who have handicapping conditions.

   D) All of the above.

The correct answer is "D." All choices apply.

80. **Norm-referenced tests:** (Rigorous) *(Skill 3.8)*

   A) Give information only about the local samples   results.

   B) Provide information about the local test takers did compared to a representative sampling of national test takers.

   C) Make no comparisons to national test takers.

   D) None of the above.

The correct answer is "B." Norm-referenced tests provide information about the local test takers did compared to a representative sampling of national test takers.

81. **If you get your raw score on a test, you will get:** (Easy) *(Skill 3.8)*

    A) The actual number of points you scored on the test.

    B) The percentage score of the number of questions you answered correctly.

    C) A letter grade for your work on the test.

    D) An aggregated score for your performance on the text.

The correct answer is "A." A raw score is the actual number correct on a test.

82. **The data coordinator of the district who is concerned with federal funding for reading will probably want to start aggregating scores immediately because:** (Rigorous) *(Skill 3.8)*

    A) The public has a right to know.

    B) By aggregating, the individual scores can be combined to view performance trends across groups.

    C) This will help the district determine which groups need more remedial instruction.

    D) B and C.

The correct choice is "D." Both "B" and "C" are correct.

83. **A standardized test will be:** (Easy) *(Skill 3.8)*

    A) Given out with the same predetermined questions and format to all.

    B) Not be given to certain children.

    C) If given out in exactly the same format with the same content, may be taken over a lengthier test period (i.e. 4 hours instead of three or two).

    D) All of the above.

The correct answer is "D." All three choices describe a standardized test.

84. **Ms. Payne is preparing for a parent teacher conference. She does all of the following EXCEPT: (Easy) *(Skill 3.9)***

    A) Collects individual child running records.

    B) Puts away all the book bags and leveled pots so the classroom will be more spacious.

    C) Puts out by each child's seat the child's weekly log and spelling folder.

    D) Sets up work samples by each child's place.

The correct answer is "B" because the teacher does not want the room to appear more spacious, but wants parents to have a feel for the book bags which indicate the primacy of reading.

85. **In terms of a balanced literacy classroom, a "leveled bin" indicates: (Easy) *(Skill 3.9)***

    A) A bin of paperback books set at the child's eye level for reading choices.

    B) A bin with books the child has selected for him- or herself.

    C) A bin with books leveled by the teacher.

    D) A bin with different reading materials, including magazines, at a child's level.

"C" is the correct answer. Only teachers or in some cases, a textbook company, can "level" books.

86. **Mr. Matthews has been told that he will have to support some special needs readers in his classroom in addition to the rest of the students. He can expect to have: (Easy) (Skill 3.9)**

    A) Gifted children who are accelerated in reading skills for their grade and age.

    B) Children who have disabilities and will need special support in accessing the content and methods he uses with the rest of the class.

    C) Children who come from native language backgrounds other than English.

    D) Children who display the capacities and needs detailed in A, B, and C.

The correct choice is letter "D." All the choices are correct.

87. **A "decodable text" is:** (Easy) *(Skill 3.9)*

   A) A text that a child can read aloud with correct pronunciations.

   B) A text that a child can answer comprehension questions about with a high percentage of accuracy.

   C) Text written to match the sequence of letter-sound relationships that have been taught.

   D) None of the above.

This is choice "A" which is the definition of decodable.

88. **Emergent literacy is:** (Rigorous) *(Skill 3.9)*

   A) An updated term for reading readiness.

   B) A stage that follows early reading.

   C) A description of children's gradual entry into reading from birth onward.

   D) A set of incremental skills that must be mastered before reading.

The correct answer is "C." The concept of emergent literacy has supplanted reading readiness in the current thinking about reading. From birth onward, children engage in behaviors that lead to reading.

89. As far as the balanced literacy movement is concerned the "WHOLE" is: (Average rigor) *(Skill 3.9)*

A) All the reading themes to be covered that day.

B) The whole class meeting for the mini lesson.

C) The complete unit to be covered over the month.

D) All of the reading and writing work to be done in connection with one book.

"B" is correct because that is the definition of "WHOLE" in balanced literacy.

90. As part of a study for a unit on the history of Massachusetts, Mr. Gentry is using the early childhood book *26 Letters and 99 Cents* by Tina Hoban. He wants his readers to study it and create a more detailed guide to their state using its concept. This is a technique frequently used in: (Average rigor) *(Skill 3.9)*

A) Reading and writing workshop.

B) Writing process instruction.

C) Readers workshop.

D) Technical writing.

The answer is "A." The fact that Mr. Gentry wants his class to use this for both reading and writing should help you pick the right choice even if you don't know the answer.

91. **A teacher is asking children to look at the beginning letters of words. She then asks the child to connect the beginning letter to the text and story and to think about what word would make sense there. This is an example of:** (Average rigor) *(Skill 3.9)*

    A) A balanced literacy approach.

    B) A phonemic approach.

    C) A phonics approach.

    D) AN ELL differentiated approach.

The correct choice is "C." The focus on letters and sounds is a phonics approach.

92. **By November the first graders have a vocabulary of words which they can correctly pronounce and read aloud. These words are their:** (Rigorous) *(Skill 3.9)*

    A) Sight vocabulary.

    B) Recognition vocabulary.

    C) Personal vocabulary.

    D) Working vocabulary.

The correct answer is "B." This describes recognition vocabulary.

93. **When teaching children to read nonfiction, the knowledge of different text structures will provide them with:** (Rigorous) *(Skill 3.9)*

    A) Predictable questions for self-correction.

    B) The fluency to promote reading speed.

    C) Skills to navigate different parts of the book

    D) Schemata that promote comprehension.

The correct answer is "D." Once a student recognizes that a paragraph or whole piece is written as a comparison/contrast, this provides a mental "map," or schemata, to aid to the student's comprehension as s/he reads.

94. **In the balanced literacy approach, ability groups are: (Rigorous)** *(Skill 3.9)*

    A) Abolished.

    B) Recommended.

    C) Mixed.

    D) Changeable.

The correct answer is "D." Unlike the Robins and Wrens of the past, ability groups are formed for relatively short periods of time (2-3 weeks to a month) and are then changed as children's skills and needs change.

95. **What is the optimum order for teaching these phonics skills? (Rigorous)** *(3.9)*

    A) Long vowels, digraphs and blends, diphthongs, short vowels, and r-controlled words.

    B) Short vowels, long vowels, digraphs and blends, diphthongs, and r-controlled words.

    C) Digraphs and blends, diphthongs, long vowels, short vowels, and r-controlled words.

    D) Short vowels, digraphs and blends, long vowels, diphthongs, and r-controlled words.

The correct answer is "D." All of the answers above presuppose that children have been taught the consonants first. Next come the short vowels because they appear in so many one-syllable words, followed by digraphs (wh-, sh-, ch-, th- and ph-) and blends (bl, cl, tr). Long vowels are followed by the more challenging concepts of diphthongs and r- and l-controlled words.

96. **The strongest purpose of an author's chair is to:** (Rigorous) *(Skill 3.9)*

    A) Give recognition to children as authors.

    B) Allow the children to hear a variety of readers.

    C) Give volunteers an opportunity to read.

    D) Give the children practice in oral expressiveness.

The correct answer is "A." Children need authentic recognition for their writing efforts, and the author's chair is a fine way to accomplish this.

97. **All of the following can be added to a root word except:** (Rigorous) *(Skill 3.9)*

    A) An affix.

    B) An inflectional ending.

    C) A compound word.

    D) A prefix.

The correct answer is "C." Two root words could be added together to make a compound word such as firefighter, but it would not make sense to add a compound word to a root word.

98. **A veteran teacher waited for her adult daughter outside of her daughter's first class in the Teaching of Reading. As she and her daughter talked about the first session of the course, the teacher never heard an explicit mention of the teaching of reading. All she heard about was:** (Easy) *(Skill 3.9)*

   A) Learning about narratives.

   B) Dealing with text structures.

   C) Constructing meaning.

   D) All of the above.

The correct answer is "C" which emphasizes "constructing meaning," a related phrase for "reading."

99. **A very bright child in a grade one class came from a family which did not a have a strong oral story telling or story reading tradition in its native language. This child would need support in developing:** (Rigorous) *(Skill 3.9)*

   A) Letter-sound correspondence skills.

   B) Schemata for generic concepts most children have in their memories and experiences based on family oral traditions and read alouds.

   C) Oral expressiveness.

   D) B and C.

The correct answer is "B." This echoes the fact that most children would have schemata based on family oral traditions.

100. **Ms. Ancess used to take time to have her children memorize major poems and even had an assembly for parents and school staff where the children dramatically recited various poems. Now that she is worried about the children's reading scores, she doesn't want to waste time with this memorization. However, if she still includes this high interest, child-centered experience:** (Rigorous) *(Skill 3.9)*

A) The children can use their oral fluency and her modeling as a bridge for enhanced comprehension.

B) The children can get a sense of "ownership" of the words.

C) The children's memory skills will improve.

D) The children's test scores will probably suffer.

Choice "A" is the best theory answer here. This activity will help the students to enhance their comprehension skills.

Constructed Response Questions (Skill 4.10)

Constructed Response Question One

Jean is a first year teacher who is taking over the classroom of a thirty-year veteran teacher who is retiring. Jean goes in to meet with the teacher. The teacher, Ms. Banks, talks about the importance of teaching the young first graders the concepts of print.

She gives Jean a list of these concepts and suggests that Jean create some assessment format so that she can be certain that all of her first graders learn these concepts. She also tells Jean that she will be volunteering her time in a neighborhood preschool program close to her home and so she will be taking her private books and materials with her. She suggests that Jean go over the list of concepts of print and consider the needs of her class as she prepares for teaching this crucial set of skills. Before Jean leaves the classroom, Ms. Banks tells her that the kindergarten teacher has let her know that three children who will be in her class next year are from ELL backgrounds where their families are not involved in oral story telling or reading from native language texts.

Ms. Banks' concepts of print list:

- STARTS ON LEFT

- GOES FROM LEFT TO RIGHT

- RETURN SWEEP

- MATCHES WORDS BY POINTING

- POINTS TO JUST ONE WORD

- POINTS TO FIRST AND LAST WORD

- POINTS TO 1 LETTER

- POINTS TO FIRST AND LAST LETTER

- PARTS of the BOOK: Cover, Title Page, Dedication page, Author and Illustrator

Jean thanks Ms. Banks for all of this help and asks if she can send Ms. Banks some of her teaching ideas for Concepts of Print and the ways she plans to differentiate instruction for her ELL students before the end of the year. Ms. Banks smiles and says she feels good to know that her classroom will be taken over by Jean. She promises to review Jean's response.

Constructed Response Answer One

First, as far as assessment for the key skills of concepts of print, I have decided that it is very important that I have a record of when and how well each of my students masters these concepts. After much thought, I realized that I will be keeping assessment notebooks for all of my students as part of my general reading and teaching. Therefore, I plan to print out all the key concepts of print on an 8" x 11" piece of paper in a grid format. This sheet will be included with other assessment grids for each individual child.

After conferencing with the child and I determine the child has demonstrated mastery of a particular concept, I will check it off on the grid and date that mastery. If I have other comments to make about the child's level of mastery or fluency, I will make an anecdotal notation about the child as well. I think that this will guarantee that I have a detailed checklist record and anecdotal record of all my children's individual progress on concepts of print.

I plan to use big books and many of the latest picture books, including Caldecott award winners in demonstrating and sharing with children many of the concepts of print. I will do much of my instruction mini-lessons. In fact I intend to use some of my own favorite alphabet books to introduce these conventions. With a book like Clare Beaton's, *Zoe and her Zebra*, I can easily and naturally cover the title page, cover, illustrator, and also manage to engage the children in the use of repetitive language.

Once I have shared that delightful book with the children as a read-aloud, we will be able to return to it again and use the repetitive language of it in its big book format to demonstrate for the children how they can point under each word as if there is a button to push. I can also demonstrate for the children how they should start at the top of the text and move from left to right. I will model going back to the left and under the previous line in a return weep.

After modeling this as part of the mini-lesson, the children can be divided in small groups or pairs and take other big book and practice the "point under each word" and the "return sweep" as part of "shared reading" or buddy reading. I should be able to identify some highly proficient readers who will be happy to serve as 'buddy" reader/tutors for the ELL children. I will ask that these "buddies" take time in small groups to work on another book from the alphabet book collection to share with the class as a whole. The use of the alphabet books also helps me to get some time in on the alphabetic principle.

I will also do a classroom writing workshop using the original alphabet book I use for the read-aloud, say *Zoe and Her Zebra* as a model for creating our own story. Perhaps we will call it *Barry and his Boxer*. In this way we will have a concrete literary product that demonstrates the children's mastery of and fluency in the concepts of print as they create an "in style of" story about a peer using illustrations, title page, dedication page, numbering of pages, back and front cover and other concepts of print.

I think that using individualized assessments, a group/class collaborative writing project, and an anchor alphabet book will help me successfully teach the concepts of print and address the needs of my ELL learners as well.

Constructed Response Question Two

Marianne has been selected as one of a team of teachers who will start teaching in a brand new school building that has been under construction for several years. While Marianne, a grade three teacher, is thrilled to be moving into new facilities, she is a bit overwhelmed to have to "set up her room" all over again at the new site. Her administrator, Mr. Adams, tells her that there are five new teachers with no previous experience teaching primary school age children who will be on staff. He tells her that these educators could really use help setting up their classrooms.

Marianne smiles and decides that she would very much like to use her set-up of her own grade three classroom as a workshop and demonstration for setting up a literacy teaching environment for these new staff members. Mr. Adams thinks that is a great idea and asks Marianne for an agenda and for a general description of what she will cover in her three hour workshop so that he can give it to the district office.

Marianne is happy to comply because she realizes that she will be assisting new colleagues and getting ten helping hands to help her set up all the materials she has accumulated over a twenty-year career.

Constructed Response Answer Two

The concept of sharing with new colleagues how to set up a classroom is very exciting to me. I know, based on my experiences, how crucial a well-planned and conceptualized space is for young learners' literacy learning. Therefore this is an agenda for what I will cover in my three hour in service session for my new colleagues.

First, I will discuss how whatever the size of the classroom space, it must be sectioned off into the following areas: a meeting area, with a sofa or "soft" setting; a chair, easel and basket to store book bags; a conference table; children's tables; and bin/basket main area for trade books; and another space for computers.
I may even give out a diagram of my classroom from my old school and some pictures. We will discuss collaboratively how I will set up my own new space as well as how they will want to set up their own spaces to allow for different uses of space within their own classrooms.

I will get into the issue of whether or not they want to have a traditional desk or use smaller tables for everyone. I think that they will need time to consider their own teaching styles in this regard. All teachers need to set up a space where they can easily confer with children and have access to individual assessment notebooks, reading folders (plus poetry/spelling, reading response, and handwriting notebooks) for all their students. I intend to show them how to prepare these folders for each child and how to store them so they can get to them when they need to make additional annotations for each child.

Given the fact that I am working with new colleagues, I suspect that this will take at least an hour and a half of our time. I am also going to model for them a weekly reading log.

Most important of all, I am going to spend the major amount of time talking to them about the book bins as I place mine around the classroom. I will show them how to label the books using the Fountas and Pinnell levels and how to arrange the book bins with the spines out so that the children can see the books. Together we will examine how the bookcases should be close to the walls and the expository books should be separated from the narrative texts. I will also get together my audio-cassettes and book sets so that they can see how I set up my read-along center for all my children. I will share some dual language tapes I use with ELL students as well. I have some extra "author's hats" and author's chair slipcovers I will share with them.

I also intend to show them how to select big books for the easel display and anchor books to be shown there as well. By the way, I will also coach them how to write away for supplies and how to store supplies in common areas so that some children are not missing necessary materials for class activities.

Even though we are focusing on literacy, I am going to show them where to store mathematics materials, other texts, and art supplies. I will end the session by making sure that they know where to place their chart wall and the word wall. If I have time, I will sit down with each of them and start them on the word wall and some key charts for their first day. They will leave my room with an actual experience of setting up a literacy environment, plus viable teaching and reading suggestions for the first day. Most importantly, I will be available for an in-school classroom consultation, if necessary.

Tips and Reflections for tackling the Constructed Response Questions:

- Use as many phrases and words from the question as possible in your response.

- Be specific. Mention specific books, authors, theorists, and strategies you have studied. Even though this is a test about the teaching of reading, make specific use of children's trade books and literature if appropriate.

- Use as many details as you are given in the question to make your response. Write no more than 5-7 moderately brief paragraphs. The more you write, the larger the margin for error. Check your spelling, grammar and check to see that you answered everything that was asked, but no more than what was asked. Be positive and proactive about your ability to respond to whichever situation is presented.

- Stick with strategies, teaching ideas, and methods that are tried and true.

- Reread your writing at least twice for spelling and grammatical errors.

Additional Professional Citations

Block, Cathy Collins. (2002). *Comprehension Instruction: Research Based Practices.* New York: The Guilford Press.

Calkins, Lucy McCormick. (2001). *The Art of Teaching Reading.* New York: Longman.

Cambourne, Briane. (2002). "Conditions for Literacy Learning." *The Reading Teacher,* 55, (8): 758-62.

Cambourne, Briane. (1993). *The Whole Story: Natural Learning and the Acquisition of Literacy in the Classroom.* Auckland, NZ: Ashton, Scholastic.

Cunningham, Patricia M. (2000). *Phonics They Use: Words for Reading and Writing.* 3rd Edition. New York: Addison Wesley Longman.

Evidence Based Reading Instruction. (2002) Articles from International Reading Association. Newark, Delaware: *International Reading Association.*

Hoyt, Linda. (2002). *Make it Real-Strategies for Success with Informational Texts.* Portsmouth, NH: Heinemann.

Kimball-Lopez, Kimberley. (1999). *Connecting with Traditional Literature.* Boston: Allyn and Bacon.

Moustafa, Margaret. (1997). *Beyond Traditional Phonics.* Portsmouth, NH: Heinemann.

Owocki, Gretchen. (2003). *Strategic Instructions for K-3 Students.* Portsmouth, NH: Heinemann.

Owacki, G, and Y. Goodman. (2002). *Kidwatching-Documenting Children's Literacy Development.* Portsmouth, NH: Heinemann.

Quindlen, Anna. (1998). *How Reading Changed My Life.* New York: Ballantine Books, 1998.

Routman, Regie. (2000). *Conversations.* Portsmouth, NH: Heinemann.

Schultz, C. (2000). *How Partner Reading Fosters Literacy Development in First Grade Students.* Action Research project, Saginaw Valley State University, University Center, Michigan.

Short, K., J. Harste and C. Burke. (1996). *Creating Classrooms for Authors and Inquirers.* Portsmouth, NH: Heinemann.

Trelease, Jim. (2001). *The Read-Aloud Handbook.* 4th Ed. New York: Penguin.

Wilde, Sandra. (2000). *Miscue Analysis Made Easy: Building on Student Strengths.* Portsmouth, NH: Heinemann.

Wilde, Sandra. (2000). *Reading Made Easy*. Portsmouth, NH: Heinemann.